Content Writing

3 Manuscripts in 1 Book, Including: How to Write Content, How to Write Non-Fiction and How to Edit Writing

Jaiden Pemton

More by Jaiden Pemton

Discover all books from the Creative Writing Series by Jaiden Pemton at:

bit.ly/jaiden-pemton

Book 1: *How to Write Fiction*

Book 2: *How to Tell a Story*

Book 3: *How to Write a Screenplay*

Book 4: *How to Write Sales Copy*

Book 5: *How to Edit Writing*

Book 6: *How to Self-Publish*

Book 7: *How to Write Non-Fiction*

Book 8: *How to Write Content*

Themed book bundles available at discounted prices:

bit.ly/jaiden-pemton

Copyright

Under no circumstances will any legal responsibility or blame be held against the publisher for any reparation, damages, or monetary loss due to the information herein, either directly or indirectly.

Respective authors own all copyrights not held by the publisher.

The information herein is offered for informational purposes solely, and is universal as so. The presentation of the information is without contract or any type of guarantee assurance.

The trademarks that are used are without any consent, and the publication of the trademark is without permission or backing by the trademark owner. All trademarks and brands within this book are for clarifying purposes only and are the owned by the owners themselves, not affiliated with this document.

Table of Contents

Book 1: How to Write Content

---

7 Easy Steps to Master Content Writing, Article Writing, Web Content Marketing & Blog Writing

Jaiden Pemton

Introduction

When it comes to content writing, it is crucial to be aware of your audience, the needs they have, and how the content you are writing can satisfy their needs and positively impact their lives. This guide will show you how to develop engaging content which will leave your readers feeling satisfied and anxious to come back for more.

In an ever-changing world, there are millions of types of content. Because of this, it can be difficult to set your content apart and prove to readers why they should engage with it as opposed to the other competitors. Within each field of content writing, you can expect hundreds, if not thousands of different perspectives, calls to action and approaches. For this reason, it is crucial to have all the necessary information, know how to talk to your audience, and develop skills that set you apart and help you to achieve the necessary amount of engagement.

This guide will explore the importance of identifying your audience, defining your purpose, and writing content that will excite them and move readers to action. You must understand the logistical necessities of content writing, such as how to present the main ideas, write your conclusion, check your evidence, and edit yourself for technicality purposes. You will also understand how to use your own passion and voice as a way to develop a following surrounding your content, and give readers the feeling of importance within your niche.

This guide will provide you with mistakes to avoid, such as being too broad or narrow, boring your readers, or getting off-topic. You will learn how to avoid cliches and answer all of your reader's questions as they read. You will discern how to check every box in terms of audience questions, concerns, and desires, showing them what they need and how your content can help them get there.

This guide has everything you need to write effective content in a comprehensive step-by-step reference format. You will be exposed to every piece of in-depth knowledge necessary to appeal to your audience, provide the right information, and present a clear call to action. Additionally, you will understand how to distinguish the content you write from other content in your niche, and develop a feeling of reliability and engagement from your readers.

The chapters of this guide will take you through each step of the content writing process to help you avoid common mistakes and develop the process that works best for you and your content. Each chapter is designed with great detail to help you stay on track and address any questions or concerns you have along the way.

Chapters are easy-to-follow with examples of tips, tricks, techniques, and things to avoid. No matter what you are aiming to advertise through your content writing, or who your audience is, this guide has all the tools you need and is sure to serve as the perfect guide to revolutionize your content writing experience.

Happy writing!

Chapter 1: Step 1 - Writing for Your Audience

When it comes to writing content, you must be specific when choosing what information will make it to the page. This decision is heavily dependent on the audience, and the purpose your content aims to fill for a particular audience. Audience interest levels will determine the sorts of statistics, facts, personal narratives, observations, testimonies, and research you should present to your readers. The way you speak about an election process to a room of second graders, for example, is much different than how you would speak about it to a high school civics class or a room of Political Science majors. Understanding the audience is crucial to determining your tone, language, and the general complexity of a particular topic. The tone you select will shape your content and serve the purpose of keeping the audience engaged.

Knowing Your Audience

When it comes to delivering your content, you must have the correct information about your audience to ensure they will be interested and impacted by what you have to say. Consider the election example again. If you are presenting information to a classroom of second graders, you will need to use simple, image-based language and put things into terms that younger children will understand. If you're writing to a high school class, you should assume they have a bit more knowledge due to more experience, but you should not assume that they are experts on the topic.

Advanced figure charts, specified jargon, etc. may not be familiar to these students and may likely end up turning them off. If you're writing for an audience of Political Science majors, you can assume they have higher levels of expertise in the topic and will be in search of more in-depth statistics and terminology. By knowing the level of knowledge, interest, and life experience your audience has ahead of time, you will be able to create much more meaningful connections with them.

Visualizing Audience Reactions

The audience—individuals who will read your content—are one of the major determining factors in how you should develop it. You must have enough information about your audience to visualize their reactions, questions, and what they expect from you. You should have an acute awareness of your reader's interests, hopes, problems, goals, and general characteristics. This knowledge is also important when it comes to digital followers, including unintended readers who may stumble across your content. While invisible readers should not be the major determining factor in the content you write, you should keep some awareness that they may come across your content.

Obtaining Audience Demographics

When it comes to gathering information about your audience, there are several elements to consider. The first element to consider is demographics. Demographics are the data that revealed factors such as age, ethnicity, gender identity, sexual orientation, religious identity, socioeconomic status, and cultural beliefs. Most content writing assignments require an understanding of audience demographics in order to determine what needs to be said and how to say it.

Considering Level of Education

Another element of audience information to consider is the level of education. This applies in the earlier example of writing election content. When audience members have a higher level of education, they will be hungry to read a formal and elevated style with in-depth information and terminology. Conversely, if you are writing to a group of high school students, you will need to be more relaxed and avoid using terms that will cause readers to get lost.

Determining Prior Knowledge

Prior knowledge is also important when deciding how to write your content. You must be aware of what the audience already knows about the topic. Are there any terms or concepts you need to define to make sure your reader understands what's being discussed? How can you feed the knowledge they already have and teach them something new, without going too far over their heads? As a content writer, it's your job to make reasonable assumptions about what your readers already know in order to avoid boring or confusing them.

Defining Reader's Expectations

Lastly, you must be aware of your reader's expectations. What will your audience expect to get out of reading this piece of content? What can they expect to learn? They may approach your content with preconceived notions about the topic and the impact they hope it will have. Additionally, they may have expectations for technicalities like grammar, terminology, formatting, and font. Be mindful of how you title your content, as this will be one of the major determining factors to shape your audience's expectations.

Determining Content Purpose

Once you have determined your audience demographics, education, prior knowledge, and expectations, you can begin to make decisions about the purpose and tone of your content. The purpose of writing a piece of content serves to answer the question "*why?*" If you are writing a piece of content about an election, geared towards an audience of college students, perhaps your purpose is persuading college students to vote. Perhaps your purpose is to create a sense of customer satisfaction in terms of readers feeling pleased with the content they engage with. Or you may seek to fill the void readers feel when they believe businesses do not accurately understand their needs. You may also seek to ease the frustration readers feel by making them feel understood and like the content they are seeing is relevant to their needs. As you develop your purpose, make sure to familiarize yourself with marketing tactics, areas of customer satisfaction and dissatisfaction, and the importance of timing.

Attracting Audience Attention

After you have developed an understanding of who your audience is and the purpose your content will serve, it's time to attract the reader's attention and keep them interested. The world is overflowing with content, and it can be overwhelming to create quality content that stands out. That said, there are a number of tips that can make you a content writing expert in no time at all.

Asking Questions and Sharing Extra Information

Your audience will not be engaged with your content if they don't feel like it is speaking to them. One of the best ways to interact with your audience is by asking questions. Statistically, asking questions of your readers makes them feel important and connected to the content. Asking questions makes readers use their brains to decide whether or not they agree with you, and if they do, this is a good sign that they are being persuaded. It can also be useful to share information about topics related to your content, which will give readers further reasons to engage. Ask yourself how you can produce content that readers will find valuable and lead them towards further action. By sharing further related topics, you can create a sense of community surrounding your audience's values and interests.

Making Use of Written and Video Reviews

Reviews are another excellent way to keep audience members excited and engaged with your content. As a content writer, you should be aware of the best services and resources within your niche, and you can use this knowledge to your advantage. You can gain credibility as a content writer by writing reviews of products, apps, services, and other resources to share information with your audience.

In doing this you can create excitement over tips, advice, recommendation, benefits, and things to stay away from. By that same token, video interviews are another trend that can help you develop yourself as a content writer. You can support the content you write by conducting video interviews where people share their thoughts on the topic at hand. If you can't do interview videos, written interviews can work just as well, and readers will enjoy gaining new information and insights from other readers in the community.

Knowing Your Niche

If you are writing for a particular audience, such as within an academic field or business niche, you should seek to share insights with your readers. What knowledge do you hold about this niche that your readers don't? Take the opportunity to share your insight, along with comprehensive lists of tips and tricks your readers will be excited to listen to. In doing this, you can establish credibility surrounding your brand, business, or topic.

That said, if your audience is broader, you should be careful with being overly specific. If you are writing content (especially website content) and are unsure of your audience's specific expertise, you should aim to maintain a simple, conversational tone. No matter who you are writing to, it's important to keep things concise. No one wants to read long sentences. The longer your sentences are, the more likely your readers are to lose sight of your purpose. It's best to keep your sentences short, clear, and to the point. If your sentences are long, try splitting them up to make them more readable.

Chapter 2: Step 2 - Assigning a Purpose to Each Paragraph

When it comes to reading content, no one likes to read large blocks of text. As previously discussed, it is crucial to maintain a sense of clarity and make your reader quickly aware of your purpose. Content writing should be broken up by paragraph, with a clear purpose and position in each. Paragraphs are designed to split the information up into easy-to-swallow sections—each focused on a single, coherent idea.

All sentences in a paragraph should support the main point. In each paragraph you write, you should establish a clear purpose (*why* this paragraph is being written), the tone (*how* you will convey the subject), and the audience (to *who* this paragraph is addressed). One of the best ways to keep yourself on track with this mission is to start a new paragraph with each new idea you introduce and run each paragraph through a "checkpoint" process.

One of the most common mistakes novice writers make is to write disjointed paragraphs that don't seem to have any relation among them. This can be highly confusing for readers. As such, the aim is to link every paragraph so that you transition from one point to another.

A good rule of thumb is to look at each paragraph as an individual point you'd like to make regarding your main idea. As such, it's a type of puzzle that you are putting together as you transition from one part of the discussion to another. Once you put all of the pieces together, you can articulate an argument that makes sense throughout the passage.

So, let's take a look at the most effective tips you can put into practice as you look to write up your content.

Creating Summary Paragraphs

One major way to condense your content and maintain purpose is by creating summary paragraphs. One of the best ways to do this is to write out all of your information, then condense it into the most important pieces. You get practice summarizing every day in your conversations in class, with coworkers, or friends by describing the major highlights, information, and purpose of what you're talking about.

Summary paragraphs work in a very similar way as you condense larger blocks of text into smaller paragraphs using only the most crucial bits of information. It is important to use your own voice as you craft your summary paragraphs, bringing your personal twist to the most important information in your content. Although it is important to keep things brief, you must make sure not to eliminate any key points or pieces of supporting evidence.

Now, it's important to be careful to not include too much information in a single paragraph. Of course, there is a great deal of value in synthesizing your points effectively. The last thing readers want is for you to go on and on when you could have gotten straight to the point. This is very useful in words of non-fiction. As for works of fiction, you need to be sure that you use the right number of words. By "right amount," we mean that you should take your time to describe points as they are intended to be described. For instance, novels require great depth when it comes to describing scenes and characters. Additionally, novels require you to be thorough when presenting a sequence of events. In the case of non-fiction works, you need to present as much information as you can in as few words as possible.

Do you see the difference?

Please keep in mind that this is a skill that can be developed over time. So, please make sure that you take the time to practice your skills so that you can sharpen them as much as possible.

Quickly Answering Reader's Questions

As you write each paragraph, it is crucial to approach the task with your reader in mind. Remember that your reader will likely be reading your content quickly, and you must respond to their needs within that time. Write the most relevant information, and write for your reader to scan the content. Make sure to conduct thorough research to provide relevant information that will answer your reader's questions and meet their needs.

In non-fiction, it is essential to address readers' questions for the get-go. Sure, you might want to take a few words to introduce the topic and build momentum. However, you will lose readers if you take too long to make your point. Readers want you to get straight to the point. After all, they are looking at your content to find value. This value comes in the form of information. This is something they cannot get if your works are filled with fluff. Naturally, getting to the point is crucial. So, try to avoid beating around the bush as much as you can. Address questions directly. Don't hesitate to economize words and lines. The most important thing is to deliver value every step of the way.

Offering Accurate Descriptions

Although it is important to be concise, you must be sure to offer thorough descriptions of your content. As a content writer, it is your job to determine the services and benefits of the content you are writing on. How can you write about the content in your niche in a way that will stick with readers? What benefits set your content apart? Before you begin to write your paragraphs, take time to make a list of the most important points you will be discussing. Play with several ideas for outlines to determine the correct order of events. How can you adequately transition from one paragraph to the next? How can you use your various research points, narrative tools, and statistics to build up to the largest purpose of the content?

Indeed, furnishing accurate descriptions is about stating the right words at the right time. Now, in novels and works of non-fiction, it might be tempting to describe people and places at length. That's fine only if it leads you somewhere. But if you drag things on for too long, you'll eventually lose readers. The idea here is to provide the right level of detail for the topic you're covering.

Consider this situation.

You are working on a technical handbook. This book requires a good level of detail as you need to accurately describe the elements making up the guide. You need to give readers as many details as possible so that they can carry out the task effectively.

Does this mean you need to write extensively on each element?

Not necessarily. What it means is that you need to ensure that your writing is clear enough so that your readers know exactly what you're talking about. Often, that comes with experience. You may not know exactly how much to write in the early going. However, the experience will show you what a reasonable level of detail would be.

A good rule of thumb is to see things from the perspective of your readers. Think about how you would feel if you were reading it. Your descriptions might make perfect sense to you, but they might not make sense to someone else. If anything, you can always ask someone else to take a look at it for you. That way, you can gauge the effectiveness of your writing.

Narrowing Down Main Points

In the case of the election content, you may decide that your main points are as follows: the statistics of college students who vote, the reasons some students feel discouraged from voting, the issues that get students to the polls, and the ultimate results of young people showing up to cast their votes. By dedicating paragraphs to each of these paragraphs you can accurately keep your reader on track and build up to the primary persuasive purpose, which is to get college students to vote.

In this example, you need to be clear about your points. Otherwise, it might be tempting for you to lose sight of your objectives. When you lose sight of your objectives, you tend to rant and wander away from your main points. This can lead to vague passages that don't address your core arguments. This is why sticking to your argument is crucial when it comes to ensuring effective writing. If you feel that a specific sentence or paragraph does not add anything to your core argument, then drop it. Please remember that there is a great deal of value in always sticking to the point. While it might seem restrictive to some degree, the last thing you want is to be overly vague.

Avoiding Passive Sentences

As you write each paragraph, it is important to survey each sentence for passivity. It is crucial to avoid passive sentences at all costs and keep things in the present tense. Content written in the passive voice is not only less engaging but also more clunky and difficult to understand. By keeping your content in the present tense, you can give readers a greater ability to understand the message and be impacted by it. Passive voice is generally employed in academic and scientific texts. So, it's important to keep that in mind as you go through your overall text.

It's also important to keep in mind that using the passive can get tricky. This is especially true if you build long and complex sentences. This is why the passive is generally limited to academic writing. If you're writing fiction, the passive should be avoided as much as possible. This is especially true if you're writing a fast-paced novel. The passive requires a lot more time to process. Therefore, a thriller needs to stay on target as much as possible.

Please bear in mind that the passive is also very impersonal. This is why it is often used in an academic tone. So, if you're looking to create a warm and inviting atmosphere, using the active voice makes the most sense. In doing so, you can keep things personal and close to your audience.

Chapter 3: Step 3 - Determining Main Ideas and Conclusion

We have discussed the importance of breaking the main ideas into paragraphs, but how do you determine the main ideas? In order to determine the main ideas from a longer passage of information, you must be able to execute a critical understanding of the information. One of the first ways to demonstrate this understanding is by reading the passage thoroughly, then identifying the topic. Who or what is this paragraph focused on? In the example with the content directed towards college-aged voters, the *who* is college-aged voters, and the *what* is the election results.

Summarizing Passages

As you seek to develop your main ideas, you must be able to summarize each passage of information. With every testimony, graphic, or piece of research you read to generate your content, you should aim to summarize it in one sentence. How would you describe the main ideas of each of the informational sources you are using in as few words as possible?

Maintaining Overarching Themes

In the search for the main idea, you should pay special attention to the introductory and concluding information. The first and last sentence of your content should make sense in the overall theme of the content, and the main idea should be expressed. In some cases, you may use the first sentence to set a precedent, then use words such as "but", "thus," or "however" to imply that the second sentence is actually where the main idea lies.

Utilizing Repetition

As you write your content, make sure to provide repetition of common ideas. As your reader reads each paragraph, they should be able to easily summarize what it is about. If they are struggling, they will immediately look for repeated words, phrases, and ideas. Therefore, it is crucial to include this repetition as a guide to keep your readers on track. This repetition leaves the reader with no question of what the paragraph is talking about.

Topic and Thesis Sentences

When the main idea is stated directly, it is called the topic sentence. It is useful to include a topic sentence in each paragraph in order to set the precedent for the rest of the paragraph. The topic sentence should provide a clear idea of what the paragraph will discuss, and it should introduce supporting details readers can look to for evidence. If you have several paragraphs on the same topic within your content, you may be better off using an overarching thesis statement, which you can divide into smaller points throughout the piece.

Implying the Main Idea

If you do not define the main idea in direct terms, you still need to imply it. This implied main idea implores readers to examine the content closely, engage deeply with it, and truly understand what you are trying to communicate. They will pay close attention to the word choice, sentence structure, and image you are painting for them, and this will help them to feel more engaged with the content.

Avoiding Main Idea Mistakes

Now you have learned how to determine your main idea and express it in your content, but there are still several crucial mistakes to avoid. Before you define your main idea, you must be sure to use your skills to summarize the main idea of what you want to express in your content. You can do this through intense research on your topic, and seeking conclusive and persuasive evidence. You must avoid being too broad with your main ideas, while still being sure to provide enough information to your readers.

Revisiting Earlier Information

As you move into the conclusion aspect of content writing, it is important to revisit your thesis or topic sentences that were used throughout. You should model your conclusion after your introduction by referring back to the main ideas and information. Re-explain the evidence, testimonies, statistics, etc. that you used to demonstrate the truth in what you said, as well as what you want the reader to do next. Remind the reader of what they have learned, how it will satisfy their needs, and the role they have in engaging with your content. The reader should have no question of what needs to be done next, and they should feel excited to do so.

Avoiding Introductory Phrases

As you begin your conclusion, it is important to avoid phrases like "in conclusion" or "in summary." Phrases like this are cliché and may cause readers to become bored. As odd as it may seem, it is perfectly appropriate to begin a conclusion without a formal introductory phrase. If you do feel the need to introduce it somehow, you should do so by directing readers back to the evidence they have just read with a phrase like "according to the evidence."

Summarizing the Overall Argument

Your conclusion should summarize your main argument in a short 1-2 sentence blurb that compiles all of the main ideas and crucial evidence you provided in your content. Explain how the statistics, testimonials, or research you provided support the mission you are calling your reader to adopt. What are the things that a particular cleaning product apart from the rest? What are the reasons college-aged students should feel inspired to vote? What insider information can readers get from your posts on the real-estate market that they can't get from competing content?

Facing Opposing Arguments

If you have presented a direct argument as a way to prove the superiority of your content, you cannot shy away from opposing arguments. You have to face the opposition head-on, acknowledge it, and prove why it is irrelevant. In the case of the election example, you may say something like "Although many college students feel defeated by the electoral college and feel that their voices do not really matter, statistics show that their votes are crucial to determining election outcomes." This is the perfect Segway into election statistics you can use as supporting evidence.

Leaving a Lasting Impact

As you draw to the end of your conclusion, you must remember that your goal is to leave a lasting impact on the reader. You should end your piece of content writing with a direct call to action and a statement that will stick in your reader's mind. In order to do this, you should make your readers think, feel excited, and feel that their opinions and efforts matter. You must show why this topic matters, and help the reader to feel the same passion as you do. The reader should have no questions about what is expected of them, or what actions they should take in order to meet their own needs or avoid unpleasantries.

You may benefit from using a "fear tactic" of issuing a warning to further motivate readers. Another tactic is to invoke an image, which will help inspire your readers towards a reality that is better than the one they currently live in. You can add to this by predicting how reality may be shaped if your ideas are implemented. If readers can clearly visualize this, they will feel more passionate to act. Additionally, you may use your final sentence to bring up a universal topic that is easy for readers to relate to.

Speaking to All Crucial Points

As you summarize your content in the conclusion, you should be sure to speak to all of the main points. If you do not take the time to revisit every point you made, you may end up weakening the stance of the content and leaving readers with a muddled image in their head. You should make an effort to provide a general overview of the main points, evidence, and calls to action.

Additionally, you must be sure not to introduce any new information in the conclusion. The conclusion should speak to each aspect of your content, nothing more, nothing less. You need to be creative in the language you use and be sure to provide a thorough recap, but you should not add any evidence or information that has not already been said. If you try to add new information, your reader may lose sight of the main points, thus weakening the overall impact of the content. If you come up with new information that you think absolutely must be added, find a place earlier in the content to add it in, as opposed to simply tacking it on to the conclusion.

Chapter 4: Step 4 - Selecting the Correct Language to Use

When it comes to the language you use in a book, it largely depends on your audience. You cannot expect to reach your audience effectively without using the right type of language. Using the right type of language goes beyond the use of correct grammar. This is about using the language to paint the picture that you want your audience to get. Thus, you need to be sure that the language you use hits home.

Selecting the correct language is about understanding the mind of your readers. As such, your choice of language depends on the factors that you want to convey to them as effectively as possible. If you do this correctly, you will get through to your audience effectively. If you don't, then you might find your audience getting confused or missing the point entirely.

Consider this example:

You are writing an academic paper. Naturally, you expect your audience to be educated individuals with college degrees. As such, it would make sense to use a very formal tone and language to present your paper. Now, imagine you did the complete opposite. You used a vibrant and informal tone. That would lead your audience to stop taking you seriously. Using this type of language would lead readers to believe that you are not a serious and credible source.

Can you see how language plays a key role in getting your message across? Please bear in mind that it's not so much what you say, but how you say it. So, let's explore the elements you need to consider when selecting the language you use in your writing.

Writing for Your Audience

The first thing you need to be cognizant of is the audience you're writing for. Knowing them means to understand who they are, where they come from, and why they would read your writing. Also, you need to know how old they are, their level of education, and what they expect to gain from your writing.

At first glance, many of these elements are pretty straightforward. For instance, if you're writing a children's book, you cannot expect to use complicated language. Depending on the age of the child, you would need to use simple language that isn't tough to understand. By the same token, a book for older kids might have a bit more complex language. Still, you would try to keep it as simple as possible.

There are times when you might have to do a little more research. This is generally the case when you write non-fiction material. Non-fiction material needs to be carefully planned. In particular, you need to know more about who your intended readers are. For example, if you're writing a how-to guide, you need to know if these are novice readers or experienced practitioners. Additionally, you might find that some of your readers are not native English speakers. Therefore, understanding complex language might be tough for them. So, you write with these folks in mind.

Knowing your audience is all about tailoring language and content to suit their needs and expectations. Therefore, it's always a good idea to take the time to reflect on who you're writing for. Doing this will save you a ton of headaches down the road.

Know Your Purpose

It is vital that you identify the purpose of your writing. In short, you must be clear about why you are writing in the first place. Ask yourself these questions:

- Am I writing to inform?
- Am I writing to persuade?
- Am I writing to entertain?
- Am I writing to create awareness?
- Am I writing to debate?

Naturally, the answers to these questions will determine the approach you choose to take with your work. For example, if you're writing to entertain, light and playful tone would serve best. Therefore, you would need to use language that reflects this tone.

Knowing your purpose is an important step in delivering the written message. This is critical in creative fiction writing. If you're telling a dramatic tale, then your tone needs to be serious and somber. If this is a horror tale, then you need to be as "creepy" and mysterious as possible. Of course, that would imply using the right type of vocabulary and sentence structure.

In case you are focused more on an academic tone, then it might be best if you considered using more complex structures such as the passive in order to reflect an impartial, third-party tone. Naturally, this requires you to be more careful with the way you articulate your ideas. Otherwise, you might run the risk of confusing folks.

Selecting the Right Vocabulary

The actual vocabulary you use is dependent on your purpose. This is highly important as knowing your purpose will enable you to make sense of what the language you need to use. Consequently, you will make the right choice when it comes to selecting the proper vocabulary.

Let's consider this situation.

You are writing a thriller. In this type of novel, you need a quick, fast-paced tempo that takes the reader through a long sequence of events in a short timeframe. Therefore, you need to be economical with your writing. So, long and drawn-out descriptions won't fly. You need to keep descriptions short and get to the point of events. To achieve this, you would need shorter sentences in which you utilize lots of synonyms. Plus, you would need to ensure you're using simple tenses and clear sentences.

If you're writing an epic novel, readers will not expect a short book. They will expect you to take them on a journey through a fantasy land. Therefore, you need to be as descriptive and explicit as possible. Here, a voluminous use of adjectives is essential to painting the proper picture you want. As such, there is no need to be economical. You can take as much time as you want to set the scene for your reader. While you might still want to keep grammar simple, it is always best to make sure that you don't skimp on the details. When it comes to novels, the devil is in the details.

As you can see, your approach depends on the type of audience, purpose, and message you want to convey. You cannot expect to make a thriller move swiftly by taking the time to stop and smell the roses. By the same token, you can't expect your audience to fully imbibe your epic tale by rushing them through the events.

Selecting the Right Tone

When we talk about "tone," we're talking about the way you choose to say things. In spoken language, the tone is about the inflections in your voice. The tone is also about the speed in which you speak, and the type of accent you place on your words.

In the case of writing, the tone is all about the level of formality you use. Also, tone pertains to the way you frame the information readers get. When you hear about tone, you often see words as "academic," "lively," "serious," and "humorous." All of these words provide an indication of where your book is headed. As such, ensuring that you have the right tone depends on how you want to present your information.

Let's assume you're writing a fiction novel. Your intended audience is young adults aged 18 to 25. Since you know your audience, you know they prefer a light and informal tone. They don't want you to use highly sophisticated words. They want you to keep it simple and to the point. This means that you choose to use commonly used words, short tenses, and mainly in the active voice. You make sure that you don't use long and complex sentences that cause the reader to overly think about their meaning. As such, you want a crisp and fast-moving read. These types of books work well for people on the go.

Now, let's assume that your targeting older readers. So, you're writing a novel that deals with the struggles of life. As such, this is a very mature topic that requires a great deal of reflection and insight. Naturally, you can't expect to have a quick-paced book. You need to take your time to properly present your point, develop your arguments, and state your positions clearly. In the end, you bring about a conclusion that makes sense to the reader. In this example, you can afford to take longer to express your point, while using more complex language and structure. After all, chances are that your readers aren't necessarily on the go. Thus, they can afford to dedicate a little more time to reading.

Ultimately, the tone is about ensuring that you build the proper atmosphere. As such, you can use it to bring the reader into the right state of mind. As you build your argument, you can then drive the point home directly and effectively.

Staying True to Your Personality

One of the hallmarks of all great writers is the ability to let their true personalities shine through. Often, this means using their real voice when writing. Some writers are witty, while others are insightful. Then, you have passionate writers, while others are straight-shooters. The fact is that you need to let your voice shine through your writing. Trying to be something you're not is a sure-fire way of getting stuck. The most prolific writers can produce a great deal of content because they don't hide who they really are.

The first step to letting your personality shine through is to write the way you think. Now, this is easier said than done. It is often difficult to articulate your thoughts in a manner that's comprehensible to others. Yet, it's important to reflect your thought process in your writing.

Consider this example.

Let's suppose you're writing a romance novel. Now, you are not a naturally "romantic" person. Instead, you're more rational and down to Earth. As such, attempting to be poetic is not something that comes naturally to you. So, if you try to be as poetic as you can, you might find it very difficult to get through your novel. In contrast, if you stick to your true self, you'll find that you can put an interesting twist into this novel.

The aim here is to give yourself a chance to be who you are. Don't pretend to be something you're not. Being authentic is about using your words to describe one particular thing. Sure, others will have a different way of describing the same thing. Nevertheless, being able to let your particular voice shine through is essential to creating the right mindset in the reader.

This is what the best writers are capable of.

They transport you to their thought process. In the end, they are able to help you navigate through the maze of thoughts and ideas that lead to the ultimate outcome. Now, readers may not agree with the outcome. However, readers signed up for the trip and not necessarily the outcome. As such, it's your job to take them through a journey they will enjoy every step of the way. You can achieve this by letting your voice shine through. Don't allow yourself to get caught in being "perfect." Unfortunately, that's what a lot of writing classes intend to teach. There is no such thing as perfection. Language is an art that's intended to reflect your individuality. So, make every effort to let that individuality manifest itself.

Chapter 5: Step 5 - Providing Evidence

One of the biggest challenges that writers face is backing up their claims. This is especially important for non-fiction writers. After all, the last thing you want to do is mislead your readers. Providing misleading information is a sure-fire way of getting yourself discredited. Thus, the challenge becomes finding the right ways to back up everything you write.

Providing evidence becomes a question of producing honest and unbiased information. Ideally, you'd be reporting facts. That way, any ideas you share have the proper backup. This will lead you to become a trusted source in your particular area of expertise. Of course, there is no question that we all have our own opinions and biases. In many cases, readers expect you to make your position evident. That is why backing up your work as much as possible is essential to ensuring that you are not just throwing things out there.

As a pro, you need to become aware of the various tools you can use to back up your claims. Mainly, these devices will provide you with the tools you need to position yourself effectively in your area of expertise. So, let's get right down to it.

Why Back Up Your Claims?

There is a difference between fact and opinion. Facts are essential to building a credible argument. Facts provide a solid means of establishing a reasonable foundation for your entire argument. If you fail to do so, your readers might dismiss you altogether. While your writing might be solid, your argument might be flimsy, at best.

So, backing up claims is essential to building a reputation in your chosen area. When you back up everything you write, you instantly vault yourself into another level. This is especially true if you're challenging common beliefs and ideas. Being able to bring forth new ideas with the right sources is a great way of creating content that resonates with readers.

For non-fiction writers, providing facts enables readers to get the right information they need. As you provide them with credible sources, your readers will come to expect the real deal from you. They will come to know that you're not just pulling ideas out of a hat. Your readers will know that you have taken the time to do the research. In the end, the information you provide is filled with valuable information they can rely upon.

As for opinions, please ensure that your opinions are also based on facts. The last thing you want is to put opinions forward that doesn't have any reasonable backing to them. While they may be perfectly logical and consistent, opinions that lack backing gets dismissed or discredited. Ultimately, your opinions won't carry as much weight as well as researched ones. So, it pays to do your homework.

Not All Sources Are Created Equal

It is very important to note that not all sources carry the same weight. Mainly, sources are only as good as their credibility. Therefore, you need to ensure that whomever you cite has the right amount of weight behind them. If you cite sources that don't necessarily have a good reputation, your claims won't be taken seriously.

In the academic world, your sources are vital to ensure you have the right kind of backing. For example, scientific journals, university publications, and peer-reviewed materials are all valid materials to choose from. By the same token, reports from the mainstream media all provide adequate support for your claims, especially when describing events.

In contrast, if you choose sources that don't have adequate backing, then you are risking the validity of your claims. Even if you're assumptions are correct, the sources you cite will discredit your work. As such, you need to make sure you have the sources in mind. For instance, if you cite conspiracy sites as opposed to reputable news agencies, your materials won't have the same level of credibility. By the same token, solid sources may lead you to fine-tune your arguments as they may provide you with ideas and information you hadn't considered. Whenever possible, do a cursory search on academic databases, scientific journals, or mainstream media sources. The better the reputation of your sources, the more credibility your work receives.

Also, quoting subject matter experts is a great way of giving your materials the credibility they need. When you use expert opinions, please make sure that the context fits the overall scheme of your materials. One of the biggest mistakes is to cite an expert only to realize that their opinion somehow contradicts your arguments. Now, if you're using a contradictory opinion for the sake of framing an argument, that's fine. However, please make sure that if you're using expert opinions to support your claims, these had better be in line with what you are trying to achieve.

Types of Sources

Let's take a look at the various types of sources you can use to support your work. Please bear in mind that you want to ensure they come from reputable places and individuals. That way, your work will have the backing it needs to be taken seriously.

Scientific Journals

If your content is academic in nature, then scientific journals make all the sense in the world. You can search for individual journals to see what articles they have published on your chosen topic. Also, you can sift through academic databases. These databases group articles on specific topics published in various journals. That way, you can get a glimpse into the type of literature that's available out there.

Now, there is one caveat to scientific journals. Journals have varying levels of popularity and acceptance. As such, journals are ranked based on their reputation, standing, track record, and quality. So, it's a good idea to do a Google search to find the best-ranked journals in your chosen area. That way, you can start with publications from those journals first, and work your way down. That way, you can be sure that your sources will be taken seriously.

Whenever possible, try to avoid citing studies and papers through the media. For example, you cite a study discussed in a newspaper article. However, it would be much more effective to seek the study itself and use that as your source. The reason for this is that you can get the information you need straight from the source. The last thing you want is to report information that's already been filtered by someone else. After all, you can't be sure that another writer shares the same opinion as you do. Therefore, it makes sense to go straight to the source.

Case Studies

Case studies are a great way to find examples of the point you are attempting to illustrate. Often, case studies provide real-world situations that demonstrate your point. Also, case studies generally show how a theory can be seen in practice. That way, you can show readers how your arguments can be seen in real life.

Another way you can use case studies is to distill key points from them. When you go through one, you can find important lessons, experiences, or concepts that you can use to get your point across. Then readers will use your case study as a means of mirroring their own assumptions. As such, a case study serves to make your point. It is a means of independently verifying what you are looking to prove.

There is one caveat with case studies. Make sure that the circumstance surrounding it is relevant to your audience. For example, if the case study was conducted in a country that's very different from that of your readers, they may have trouble relating to the situation surrounding it. So, please ensure that case studies are as relevant as possible to your readers.

Testimonials

Testimonials can be a bit tricky to use, especially if they don't come from the most credible sources. In particular, testimonials from regular folks work well with advertising. However, if you're looking to back your materials, you might be better off using expert opinions.

When you use a testimonial, you need to be careful about the specific topic you're discussing. For example, if you're talking about a highly scientific topic, then you might be better off sticking to academics and subject matter experts. Now, if you're reporting facts about a specific event, then definitely witness accounts and testimonials from people directly involved are very good places to start.

In the end, testimonials can serve to prove a point, especially when you don't have first-hand knowledge of the situation. First-hand accounts very useful when you're writing a journalistic piece. As for works of fiction, you might be able to incorporate these testimonial accounts within the overall scope of the story. The main point here is to ensure that you maintain credibility. Some authors like to clarify the fact that they are presenting witness accounts and not expert testimony.

On the subject of expert testimony, such accounts from experts during court proceedings, congressional hearings, or sworn statements are all good sources of information. Since these opinions are given under oath, the individuals who furnish them need to be as forthcoming as possible. Unless these expert witnesses flat-out lie, you can be sure that you have a trusted source of information.

News Reports

You need to be careful when it comes to the media. It's important to note that the media doesn't always get it right. Of course, there are trusted publications that have an impeccable reputation. However, that doesn't mean that their work is absolutely perfect. Whenever you use journalistic works are your sources, it's always a good idea to make sure you double-check whatever is stated in their publications. It could be that news reports leave out something important or perhaps miss and key point. As such, you want to make sure you double-check. Otherwise, someone might call you out on your claims. Needless to say, that is something that you want to avoid.

When you look at journalistic works, always try to verify their sources. If you see things such as "a source spoke on a condition of anonymity" then you're dealing with hearsay. While the outlet might be reputable, the information itself cannot be independently verified. Therefore, that opens the door to unnecessary scrutiny. This is why it's always important to verify the information yourself before confidently using it in your material.

Interviews

If you have access to experts and witnesses, you can use interviews as a means of backing up your work. Ideally, you would have full permission from the individual to use their accounts freely. That way, you can use their name as a means of backing up your claims. Most experts are willing to do interviews free of charge. However, you would need to be patient and as transparent as possible.

If you use second-hand interviews, it's always a good idea to contrast the same information from as many sources as possible. Often, media edits interview to fit their airtime or particular agenda. As such, finding unedited versions whenever possible is always a good way of ensuring the quality of the information you present.

Please ensure that you avoid taking interviews out of context. This is rather easy to do, especially when you have a specific bias that you want to pursue. Unless the overall interview fits your narrative, it's always best to be fair. Taking statements out of context can seriously damage your credibility and reputation. Therefore, try your best to use the types of materials that fit your narrative so that you can maintain a consistent narrative throughout your materials.

Chapter 6: Step 6 - Triple-checking Technicalities

Quality is crucial when producing effective materials. In addition to appropriate tone, vocabulary, descriptions, and arguments, you want to ensure that you have the right grammar, spelling, and cohesion. All of these elements are fundamental to producing high-quality content.

Much of this process is done in the editing phase of your content. Editors can help you spot inconsistencies in your arguments, paragraphs, or ideas. Editing is not meant to bash your work. Instead, it's meant to clean it up so that your ideas truly shine through. Otherwise, you could find yourself making needless mistakes.

It's also worth noting that polishing up writing shows readers that you care about them. After all, if you take the time to make sure your work is spic and span, they will feel that you are serious about your work. Naturally, it doesn't matter how good your writing is. If you're sloppy, readers will call you out on it. So, it makes sense to pay attention to detail as much as possible.

So, let's take a look at how you can triple-check the finer points of your writing. In the end, you want to make sure that you put your best foot forward. This will make you seem like the real pro that you are.

Checking Grammar

Grammar is one of the trickiest parts of writing. While there is no question that you can speak the English language appropriately, using proper grammar in writing can lead you to feel out of place at the time. After all, it's one thing to have a conversation, while it's another to write down your ideas clearly and appropriately.

So, checking grammar is crucial to ensuring the right type of material you want others to see. For example, verb tenses can be tricky at times, especially when you're building long, complex sentences. Naturally, it's easier to keep it simple. When you do so, you ensure that you're not making things harder on yourself. In the end, keeping sentences short and clear is always the best way to go.

You ought to be the first line of defense with grammar. You must take the time to ensure that you're using the proper form every time. However, human error is quite possible. It could be that you simply make a mistake. Therefore, the second line of defense is useful. You can enlist grammar-correction software to help you navigate this part. Grammar-correct software uses artificial intelligence to ascertain proper writing. This type of software gets it right most of the time. Of course, it's not perfect. Yet, it can work pretty well on its own.

Lastly, getting an editor to go through your work is highly recommended. Now, you don't need to employ a professional editor or proofreader. Often, a friend or family member can help you spot things you might have missed. As such, it is always a good idea to get another pair of eyes to go through your writing. That way, you can be sure that you're getting things triple-checked effectively.

Ensuring proper vocabulary

By "proper vocabulary," we're not talking about cursing. Instead, we're talking about using the right words you need to get your point across. Many times, the right vocabulary may be technical in nature. In such cases, you might need to get someone specialized to have a look at your content.

There are other times when you might need someone to double-check the way you use specific words. For example, you might use one word or phrase too often. Therefore, having someone else go through your text would reveal such inclinations. In the end, the other person going through your text can help you find other ways of phrasing your ideas.

Proper vocabulary also refers to things use as the use of prepositions, conjunctions, and interjections. These words may be easily corrected by spellcheck software. However, it's worth noting that no software is perfect. Therefore, it's important to have a pair of human eyes to go over your text. This is how you can triple check your efforts.

If you're not confident in software, you can always have two different people go over your text. Sometimes, having two completely different individuals review your text can provide you with a good sense of how well written your text is. The idea is to be as thorough as possible. Being thorough is all about ensuring that the words you are using are being used in the proper context.

Beware of Sounding Smart

A common mistake is attempting to sound smart. This action refers to using words, phrases, and structures that make your writing more intricate than it has to be. Now, there is nothing wrong with using a formal or even academic tone if the situation warrants it. However, it is entirely different when you take a regular text and try to make it sound more complex than it should be. Many times, this is the result of feeling insecure about your writing abilities. Naturally, writers attempt to overcompensate for their perceived lack of originality or talent. However, that could not be farther from the truth. The aim is to let your voice sound true as much as possible.

When you think about your content, it's crucial to write for your audience. Thus, it's critical to avoid trying to impress your audience. When you try to impress others, you get away from your strengths. As such, you won't give yourself the proper opportunity to let your voice manifest itself.

To avoid this situation, try your best to have others judge your writing. The idea of judging is not to "pass" or "fail" your work. The aim is to have others see if your work is a true reflection of who you are. From there, you can feel confident in your ability to make your voice manifest.

Use Beta Testers

The term "beta testing" refers to running real-life trials with a finished product. The aim of a beta test is to determine how real customers react to a specific product. In the end, customer feedback is used to make any final tweaks to the product prior to its final launch.

Beta testing is very common in the software world. However, you can use it for your writing, as well. Conducting this type of testing is quite straightforward. All you need to do is to take your writing and have other folks read it.

That's all.

Then, you offer them the opportunity to critique your work. You can offer them the opportunity to provide you with freeform feedback or a more structured approach such as filling out a worksheet. Either way, your beta testers can offer you insight into the effectiveness of your writing. This feedback can give you a sense of how well you've used vocabulary, terminology, and tone. This type of testing goes beyond the mere act of double-checking grammar and spelling. This is about understanding how well your work resonates with your intended audience.

Please remember that a combination of machine and human intelligence is a great way of polishing up your writing. However, please make sure you don't take things personally. Many times, writers take critique personally. Many times, there is nothing personal. It's just a question of people providing you with an honest take on the impact your writing causes. Ultimately, you always have the opportunity to go back to the drawing board to perfect your work.

Chapter 7: Step 7 - Utilizing Your Passion and Your Voice

Passion is one of the elements that cannot be taught. Passion is all about making your voice manifest throughout your writing. This is the ingredient that great writers are able to make manifest in their work.

When you think of the best writers in history, they are all able to let their true voice shine through regardless of the topic in their writing. For example, great novelists can take seemingly pedestrian events and turn them into great works of literature. Other incredible writers can take run-of-the-mill topics and present them in a lively and entertaining manner.

Making your passion evident is far easier when you actually feel passionate about a topic. But what if you're not really into a topic? What if you're merely writing because you need to? Think of all those school papers you've had to write. How passionate were you about those papers?

Using your voice to manifest your passion is crucial in making your writing stand out above the rest. Your passion is what takes readers on a journey through the various elements needed to go from good to outstanding.

So, let's take a look at how you can use your passion to make your work stand out above the rest.

Make Your Position Clear

When you attempt to make your passion manifest, you must state your position clear. Sometimes, that means taking sides in a debate. Other times, that means staying neutral. The point here is that you want to let your readers know where you stand from the get-go. You can't reasonably expect your readers to take part in your passion if you flip-flop from one position or another.

Let's consider a couple of examples.

First, you're writing an academic work. In this work, you can state your side of the debate. You are forthcoming about your opinions, thereby leading the reader to know what side you're supporting. Also, it could be that your position is to remain neutral, that is, you're not supporting any side in the debate. As such, you present facts, state an argument, and then state conclusions based on your findings. This is a common practice among academics.

Second, you're writing a work of fiction. To make your work that much more personal, you openly take a position as part of your book's narrative. So, you let your narrative reveal what position you have taken. For instance, you're writing a romance novel in which there are clear heroes and villains. Also, you're writing a historical novel in which you seek to expose the wrongdoing of certain individuals in a series of events.

In both cases, you are presenting your position directly to the reader. The difference lies in the way you do it. When writing non-fiction, you can afford to get straight to the point. In fiction writing, you have the luxury of taking the time to get to the point. In either case, the idea is to ensure that you have a clear mindset as you write.

Avoid Becoming a Cheerleader or a Critic

When passion becomes manifest, it can be easy to get carried away. Mainly, you might find yourself singing the praises of a person or events, while you might bash other folks or situations. While we're not advocating that you always remain neutral, it's important for you to state your opinion with a clear and level-headed approach.

Let's consider both sides of the equation.

Firstly, when you favor a specific position, it's vital to state your support and then outline the reasons why you support this position. Then, it's essential to back up your supporting points. Otherwise, you may come off as a cheerleader. Of course, people who agree with your position will be happy to follow along. However, those who do not agree with you might become turned off. Therefore, you want to avoid turning people away. Doing so needlessly risks losing readers.

Secondly, when you oppose a specific position, take the time to explain why you don't favor your position without resorting to needlessly bashing your object of criticism. When you open bash other people and positions, you might come off as bitter or resentful. Needless to say, that is not what you want to portray. If you're clearly opposed to one thing or another, it's essential that you state why you oppose the situation with a clear and consistent argument.

Maintaining a level-headed approach is often hard for professional writers. Allowing your personal bias to remain clearly away from your statements is a must. Therefore, you must ensure that whatever you write, you are always on the same track. Most of all, you need to ensure that your statements and claims are fundamentally true. Otherwise, you risk becoming discredited.

Writing for Fun

For some, writing is a job. For others, writing is a passion, a hobby, a pastime, if you will. For people who truly enjoy writing for the love of it, writing comes a bit more naturally. Writing for fun then becomes an enjoyable task. This is something that often comes through in your words. Unless you write on a topic you hate, your general enthusiasm will peer through your overall work. Readers will be privy to your passion for writing.

This is a rare treat for most readers.

Think about reading the news. Journalists are often detached from the information they report. They merely stick to the facts. Moreover, journalists have templates and formats they follow to ensure they are accurate in their reporting.

Now, compare a run-of-the-mill news report to an editorial. In an editorial, you'll find the writer is truly passionate about the opinions they present. While they may try to remain objective and professional about the position they take, these writers clearly manifest their passion. They do so because they enjoy what they write. To them, writing is an exercise in self-expression.

So, look at writing as a means of expressing your personal individuality. Your readers will come to know the real you from the way you use words to express yourself. Perhaps you might not be the most articulate speaker, but you can definitely use the power of written words to make your readers jump into your psyche.

If you approach writing as a job, please be sure to find a system to help you automate your writing process. There are plenty of courses and systems out there. However, we're going to talk about one approach that's highly successful.

First, begin by briefly introducing your topic. A short background description is enough to give readers a glimpse of what they can expect in the text. This will enable readers to prepare their minds for the upcoming discussion.

Then, state your position. Try to be as clear and objective as possible. Try to avoid using colorful language that makes you a cheerleader or a critic. Also, try to avoid any inflammatory or overly enthusiastic remarks early on.

After, let your readers know that you will present your supporting evidence for your position. Whether it's a work of fiction or non-fiction, you can take the rest of your content to fully develop your argument. As you do so, make sure that you clearly outline your position as logically and consistently as possible. Please try avoiding leapfrogging from one point to another. This will only confuse readers.

Lastly, provide a conclusion in which readers can get a summary of what you have just told them. The practical purpose of this conclusion is to give readers something they can take away with them. From there, you have used a system that you can automate every time you write.

Please keep in mind that writing ought to be an enjoyable process most of the time. If you find it tough to write, don't sweat it. Often, it's a question to find the right time and mindset to produce content. The most important thing is to dedicate time to writing. In the end, you'll be able to produce your very own works much faster than you could have ever imagined.

Conclusion

When you started this guide, you likely had a product or service you were interested in advertising through content writing, and you had the desire to set yourself apart in the content writing industry. You were likely aware of all that is at stake in making your content stand out and motivating your readers, especially in a society that is brimming with new content at every turn.

Throughout the guide, you were provided with the ins and outs of the content writing process, from how to determine your audience, to maintaining engagement, making the main points stand out, introducing and concluding effectively, answering reader's questions, developing clear calls to action, and double-checking technicalities. You learned tactics for remaining consistent and reliable and building a name for yourself through your unique passion and voice.

You learned the benefits of building a community surrounding your content and making readers feel involved and important. and your content by creating a community. You learned how to address common questions and concerns to further develop your credibility and reassure your audience as they engage with the content you write. You became aware of the most common mistakes to avoid, such as being too broad, too narrow, introducing irrelevant information, or forgetting to revisit important points.

You learned how to acknowledge what your readers need, what makes them feel satisfied, and what inspires them to act. Additionally, you learned what kinds of language to use when addressing unique groups, and you developed tactics for keeping readers from getting confused or bored halfway through.

This guide has helped you discover how to capture and maintain reader engagement, as well as how to increase levels of excitement and inspiration in your community of readers. Throughout your content writing journey, this guide is sure to serve as your toolbox to guide your every move.

So, the time has come for you to go out there and show what you're capable of. Indeed, becoming a proficient writer is a question of time and practice. Nevertheless, you have everything you need to get started on your path to perfection. With each passing line and paragraph, you will perfect your craft. Eventually, you will be able to reflect your voice clearly and effectively. Your readers will come to appreciate your contributions.

Ultimately, you will discover that writing is an action that involves joy and satisfaction. Finding your inner voice is crucial to transmitting the message you want people around you to hear. As you develop your own voice, your readers will become attached to your specific brand of writing. This is what differentiates the best writers from the rest of the pack!

Book 2: How to Write Non-Fiction

7 Easy Steps to Master Creative Non-Fiction, Memoir Writing, Travel Writing & Essay Writing

Jaiden Pemton

Introduction

Welcome to "How to Write Non-Fiction". In this guide, we are going to explore how to create an exciting and engaging narrative that will captivate your readers. In particular, we are going to discuss how you can write effectively so that your readers can find your content easily digestible.

You see, the difference between good writing, and great writing, is in the way you get your message across. Many times, getting your message across is about putting yourself in your reader's shoes. When you do this, you're able to transport your readers straight into your state of mind. This is what creates an authentic reading experience.

Now, most people believe that writing non-fiction is about using academic-style prose. As such, the aim is to sound smart. This is why many non-fiction writers try their hardest to sound as smart as they can. However, this is a misconception. You don't need to sound "smart" to be a successful non-fiction writer. All you need to do is transmit the enthusiasm you have for your chosen topic. Then, you can create compelling writing that will leave readers wanting more.

In each of the chapters in this guide, we'll look at a major step in the creative writing process. It's important to note that each step builds on the previous one. In the end, you will have a winning formula once you put them all together. You will learn a successful system that has been proven to work time and time again.

So, what are you waiting for?

Let's get started with this journey into a world filled with exciting moments. After all, writing should be an enjoyable process. It should be the type of endeavor that will leave you feeling happy and satisfied with the type of content you are able to produce. Plus, you surely have something to share with the world.

That's what makes writing such a rewarding experience.

Please don't look at writing as a job. If you do so, it will become a chore, a burden if you will. As such, please take the time to go through each of the steps in this guide. You will find that writing will become one of the most rewarding and satisfying experiences you can even engage in.

Please bear in mind that the most successful writers are the ones who can convey their passion for a given topic. This passion is transmitted through their keen sense of communicating their thoughts and ideas. The best part is that this is a skill that can be developed. Therefore, anyone can develop the skills needed to be a successful writer.

Happy writing!

Chapter 1: Step 1 - Deciding on Your Narrative

All great books tell a story. Now, you might think that type of approach is reserved for fiction writing. After all, fiction is, by definition, telling a story. While this is completely true, you will find that telling a story is not just reserved for fiction. Non-fiction works can also tell a story. In fact, non-fiction writing should tell a story. The reason for this is the need for creating a narrative.

When you write in the non-fiction domain, you must strive to create a consistent narrative that can deliver meaning and value to readers in an enjoyable format. This implies that you must avoid sterile discussions. Such discussions leave readers lacking a personal touch throughout the content. Therefore, it is essential for you to find a consistent narrative that reflects your true self.

In this chapter, we are going to look at the elements you need to create a consistent narrative that will enable you to engage readers in such a way that your content resonates with them. Best of all, you will find that you don't need exceptional skills to make this type of approach perfectly plausible.

Finding Your True Voice

Often, you hear writing coaches tell their students they need to find their true voice. However, that is vague, especially if you don't know how to bring your inner voice out. Finding your inner voice is about channeling your personality. When writing, you don't need to pretend to be someone you're not.

This is one of the biggest mistakes that novice writers make.

You see, novice writers attempt to sound smart and sophisticated. This approach leads them to labor through writing tasks as they search for complex vocabulary and grammatical structures. The truth is that readers don't expect to find uber-complex language when they pick up a book. In fact, many readers simply want an enjoyable read that will leave them with the information they seek.

Here is a great exercise you can do to help you find your voice.

When you set out to write on any given topic, sit down, and write. Just write. Don't think about what others will think. Just write down your ideas. You can write as much or as little as you like. A good starting point on one page.

Once you've written your first page, stop and read it. When you read it, you will get a glimpse of the way you sound, that is, your inner voice. Of course, you would have to clean it up. After all, it is extremely rare for a writer to produce flawless content on the first try. The aim here is to simply become comfortable with your own voice.

Then, take the time to write more and more. As you write, pay attention to the type of words you use. Also, check out the type of sentences you build. You will immediately find a consistent pattern. This is your voice. As you uncover your voice, you will need to take care of appropriate grammar, spelling, and vocabulary. This is especially important if you're writing on a technical topic.

These first few pages may never see the light of day. They may remain filed away in your computer forever. However, they are the beginning of your journey as a writer. They will serve to help you find your voice. The most important thing to keep in mind is that you're not writing to please others. You're writing to get a message across.

All About Grammar, Spelling, and Vocabulary

Letting your hair down is a major step toward becoming a successful writer. However, you must ensure that you follow the proper grammatical guidelines of the English language. Of course, there is a place for certain devices such as the use of slang or informal expressions. Nevertheless, you must ensure that you use the proper vocabulary and expressions you need based on your chosen topic.

When it comes to grammar, it is important to make sure that you're using the right verb tense and sentence structure. Please keep this in mind as grammatical mistakes are the first thing that people will call you out on. Such mistakes might turn off some readers. Others may dismiss your writing entirely. While it is possible to have a mistake at some point, too many mistakes will definitely get you in trouble.

So, it's a good idea to enlist the help of an editor. You can get a trusted friend or family member to go over your writing. If you would rather get an objective third-party, you can hire a freelance editor to give your writing a look. You can find them on sites such as Fiverr. Also, you can use editing software to double-check your work. In the end, the software can help you pinpoint mistakes that you may not have caught.

As for spelling, word processing software generally checks this for you on the fly. As such, you can rely on your word processor of choice to give you a hand. In case you in doubt, a good old-fashioned dictionary will come in handy. Often, there are words and terms that even sophisticated software does recognize. So, it makes sense to have a handy reference guide. That way, you can be sure that you're getting the right spelling. If you happen to use words from other languages such as Latin or Greek, always take the time to double-check the terms. That way, you can be sure you're right on the mark.

Regarding vocabulary, please ensure that you have the right terminology. This is particularly important if you're writing on a technical subject. Often, there are specific terms that you may not be sure about. Also, things might get confusing with definitions. As such, it's always good to review that you're using the right definitions and interpretations of words.

Finding the Right Pace

Non-fiction writing can be tricky in terms of pacing. It can be quite tough to find an appropriate pace. After all, you run the risk of moving along too fast or moving along too slowly. When you fail to find the appropriate pace, readers may feel they are not getting their money's worth.

Think about it along with these terms.

In non-fiction writing, it is essential that you get to the point. Sure, you can write short introductions to present the topic. However, the sooner you get to the point, the better. When you're exploring a specific topic, the last thing you want is to drag out explanations and descriptions. Often, it's best to limit the length of definitions and focus more on examples. Also, descriptions need to be as concise as possible.

The biggest temptation here is to provide lengthy and elaborate explanations. While providing details is certainly useful, there is a limit to the level of detail you need to provide. Granted, there are topics that require a high degree of detail. In such cases, your experience and intuition will tell you how detailed you need to be. After all, you're the expert on the topic. Nevertheless, it's always best to keep things as simple as possible.

It is also important to consider your audience. Depending on the people you're writing for, you might need to slow down or speed up. For example, if you're writing a guide for beginners, you might want to slow things down and provide a greater level of detail. If you're writing a guide for experienced users, then you can certainly move along quicker.

A good rule of thumb here is to check out other books and content similar to what you are looking to produce. By comparing these other materials, you can get an idea of what works and what doesn't. That can provide you a good yardstick by which to measure your own writing. In the end, there is nothing wrong with drawing comparisons when you're new to writing.

Over time, your experience and intuition will provide you with the proper feel for the pacing you need to keep throughout your book. Moreover, you'll know where to slow down, when to pick things up, and when to really drill down.

Please bear in mind that your inner voice should make itself manifest. This means that your voice will be the reflection of your knowledge and experience. Ultimately, you can provide readers with an adequate sense of your mastery of the topic. That will produce a sense of security among your readers. They will come to recognize you as an authority on the subject.

Maintaining a Consistent Narrative

Please keep in mind that building a consistent narrative is essential in successful writing. For example, if you have a clear position on an issue, make sure you maintain this position. Flip-flopping on issues will most likely confuse your readers.

When you write guides or how-to materials, it's always a good idea to maintain consistent use of tone, grammar, vocabulary, and pacing. For instance, using complex vocabulary with an academic tone at the beginning of the book and then shifting to an informal tone with the use of slang, later on, will serve to create an inconsistent dynamic in your book. Therefore, maintaining a consistent narrative through your materials will lead readers to feel comfortable with your writing. In the end, they will come to trust you as they get a clear glimpse into your psyche. Ultimately, this will create the right environment for the materials you want to present to your readers.

Chapter 2: Step 2 – Defining Your Purpose

When setting out to write, you must find your purpose. There must be a clear purpose for your writing. Otherwise, your content might come off as a rant with no clear direction. Naturally, that's the last thing you want to get across. Therefore, your writing needs to convey a clear message. When you do that, your readers will derive value from your words. In the end, your writing becomes a valuable source of knowledge and information.

In this chapter, we are going to look at finding your purpose. This is one of the most crucial elements any time you set out to write. When you have a clear purpose, writing becomes that much easier. As such, your inner voice will manage to find its way through to your audience in a clear and easy-to-follow manner.

How to Find Your Purpose

The first question you need to ask yourself is "why?" Generally speaking, you need to ask yourself why you are setting out to write. The answer to this question will reveal the type of approach you need to take. For example, some professionals set out to write a book as a means of positioning themselves in their chosen profession. Others write because they feel it's a way of letting their feelings out. Others write because they feel passionate about an issue. Therefore, they feel that writing about that issue will raise awareness of it.

Regardless of your specific purpose, you must ask yourself why you want to write in the first place. From there, you can derive the approach you need to get your message across. Consequently, your message is the second step in this process. You must ask yourself what your message is. This concept boils down to figuring out what you want your readers to take away from your materials.

Once you have your purpose and message clearly defined, the last step is to determine your audience. This is essential as the tone of your writing needs to reflect your audience. Naturally, writing for a younger audience would require you to use a more youthful and informal tone. In contrast, writing for an older audience would require a more formal tone.

Ultimately, your approach will depend on all three factors outlined here. By taking the time to think about them thoroughly, you will make the actual writing process easier for you.

Types of Purposes

There are different types of purposes for writing. Understanding them will give you a good idea of what approach you can take. So, let's discuss them in greater detail.

Writing to Inform

This is the type of writing you can use to present information on any given topic. When you write to inform, you are simply presenting facts and information. For example, you can write a how-to guide, describe historical events, or simply discuss an issue. Ultimately, you want to maintain a neutral position, especially if you want to spark debate among readers.

Writing to inform is also about making sure you get the fact straight. Therefore, accurate information is a must. This also means getting definitions and terms right. Moreover, you want to make sure that you know your audience. That way, you can tailor your style to suit the age and background of your readers.

Writing to Persuade

There are times when you write to get a specific point across. In such cases, your point might be to persuade your readers on a position in a given issue. Thus, you need to present a convincing argument based on the facts you present. Generally speaking, writing to persuade requires an engaging tone that's meant to awaken your reader's interest. In this type of writing, using creative descriptions is always best. Having a deep level of detail is essential to defeating any qualms your readers might have. In the end, your argument is so convincing that readers will be swayed in your direction.

Writing to Raise Awareness

When you write to raise awareness on an issue, you need to communicate a specific sense of urgency. There are cases in which you want to address an extremely urgent matter. Hence, you need to cut straight to the chase. Very little introduction or background is needed. What readers expect in such cases is a quick rundown of facts. These facts are intended to highlight your position. As such, there will be no denying the importance of the issue you discuss. Here, a quick, fast-paced approach is a must.

Writing to Advertise

Some materials are intended to advertise a product or service. With these materials, it's important to underscore a problem and then show how the product or service provides a solution. Often, companies write books and papers on the most pressing issues for their customers. Then, products and services are presented as a solution to these issues. In the end, the company closes with a call to action. Readers are then compelled to learn more about the company's solutions to their problems. This type of writing needs to be persuasive and filled with actionable information readers can use to find a solution to their needs.

As you can see, the various types of writing can help you create valuable materials. Depending on your specific purpose, you might end up with a combination of all of these approaches. The main thing to keep in mind is your main purpose and the message you're looking to get across.

Getting the Right Message Across

All too often, writers get sidetracked and lose sight of their message. As such, it is essential that you keep your eyes on the prize at all times. Once you define what your message is, you need to make sure that comes across.

Let's look at an example.

You're a professional that aims to write a white paper outlining your customers' biggest problems. Therefore, your purpose is to inform, but also to advertise. As such, you want to list your customers' problems in a clear and direct manner. Something like a "top 5" or the "Three Biggest Problems" works very well to pique readers' interest. As you go through each problem, the idea is to be neutral. You want to avoid creating a negative feeling in the mind of your customers. If you do, they won't look at your products as a solution. They will look at your products as a result of the problem.

Next, outline how your product can help your customers solve their problems. Now, you want to be careful not to make any outrageous claims. But you do want to present your argument in a way that all readers can see the benefits of your product. Here, you want to provide a solid level of detail. That way, the virtues of your product will become evident.

Lastly, close out with a call to action. Something like, "visit our website to learn more" is a great way of moving from an informative approach to a selling one. In the end, your readers will find value in the information you provide, while also leading them to purchase your products.

In this example, we have a combination of writing to inform and persuade. Naturally, you want your readers to purchase your product. However, keeping a neutral and informative tone is a great way of helping your future customers see the value of your products. Otherwise, you might turn some customers off if they see you're simply peddling something.

Always Stay Positive

Keeping a positive attitude is always critical. Even if you're dealing with serious issues like climate change, you still want to maintain a positive mindset. Sure, it's important to stress the importance of serious issues. Nevertheless, attempting to evoke fear or outrage in our audience will only take you so far.

Think about this situation.

A pest control company writes a brochure about their services. The company goes on about how termites can destroy a house. If customers don't act quickly, pests might bring their house crashing down.

On the surface, that looks like effective marketing. However, customers may seek this company out of fear. In the end, customers will associate the company with a negative feeling. To maintain a positive attitude, the company can list the dangers that termites pose to a house. As such, the company is the leading source for pest control services. Ultimately, this company has the solution to any type of problem.

Do you see the difference?

The aim is to inform you about a problem by listing the potential dangers. The idea is to provide accurate information and not create panic. Then, the company presents its services as the ultimate solution to the problem. As a result, the company is associated with a solution and not the result of a terrible situation.

Please keep in mind that maintaining a positive attitude at all times is the best way for you to ensure that you're writing is always associated with positive feelings. Unless you're writing a horror novel, you should always strive to have your readers associate your content with positive feelings. This will ensure that your readers get valuable information while you position yourself as a leading source in your chose field. That's the best approach you can use to keep your readers on your side.

Chapter 3: Step 3 - Determining your Audience

A critical aspect of effective writing knowing who will read your materials. Successful writers are keen on adapting their writing style to suit whomever their intended audience is. This makes it easier for them to communicate with readers.

Knowing who your audience depends on a few key factors. That is why this chapter is all about determining what your audience is. Moreover, you will find that once you figure out who your audience is, you can tweak your style as needed.

So, let's jump right into it!

It Starts with the Topic

The starting point should always be your topic. The topic itself will tell you quite a bit about the audience you'll be catering to. This is important to note as not everyone is interested in the same topics. For example, if you're writing a knitting guide, chances are you're not going to attract many guys. By the same token, a car repair book would not attract too many ladies. Now, this isn't to say that these topics are gender exclusive. What we are saying is that certain topics cater to one specific group of people more than another.

Of course, there are cross-cutting topics that everyone would be interested in reading. For instance, books on saving money are always popular regardless of people's specific demographics. The point here is to ensure that that you have a good idea of who would be interested in reading your content.

Also, please keep in mind that some topics are considered "niche" topics. These topics cater to a very specific group of individuals. As such, these groups possess very clear characteristics that you need to consider. A good example of this is sports. While sports, as a whole, are generally quite popular, individual sports may become niche topics. After all, how many fans does curling have compared to soccer? These are considerations that you must take into account when determining your audience.

Age and Gender

One of the most important aspects to consider is age. Naturally, some topics are more attractive to younger people than to older folks, and vice-versa. You can figure out what topics folks are interested in by doing an online search. You can search for something like, "most popular books teens" to uncover what types of topics are trending among teenagers.

Also, going on online platforms such as Amazon can reveal what types of books are most popular. There, you can see the topics that most readers are into. That should give you an indication of the types of readers your content can resonate with.

As for gender, there are specific topics that resonate with males more than females and vice-versa. As such, some common sense can go a long way with this demographic. However, you might be surprised to find that some topics have cross-cutting appeal. These are topics that would interest people from all walks of life. Topics such as health and fitness, finance, and self-development all have cross-cutting appeal. Nevertheless, you will find more gender-specific topics even within the broader scope of such topics.

Tone and Approach

When putting pen to paper, your readers' level of education plays an important role in determining the type of prose you aim to utilize. In this regard, you need to determine if you're writing for a general audience or a more specific one. In the case of academic publications, you need to maintain a tone consistent with more complex and abstract language.

However, if you're writing for a general audience, you might want to keep a more standard tone. By the same token, general audiences appreciate a more neutral tone, that is, using gender-neutral pronouns while avoiding any direct references to specific characteristics otherwise required in the topic. For example, you can address your readers directly by saying "you," while avoiding gender-specific pronouns like "he" or "she." In such cases, you can opt for the use of "they."

A good rule of thumb to keep in mind is to sound as natural as possible. If you normally speak with a more laid-back tone, then that should be your default tone. Also, if you're more inclined to speak in a formal tone, then make sure you get that message across, too. The main idea here is to avoid trying to be someone you're not. Often, this is the biggest mistake that novice writers make in the early going. Your natural voice will surely resonate with your target audience quickly and easily.

Leveraging Social Media

Social media is the place to be now if you want to know what's in, and what's out. Being relatively active on social media can give you the opportunity to see what's trending. Also, you can stay up to date with the latest news and information. As such, you can leverage social media to get a great idea of how your potential readers react to specific situations.

If you already have a following, then social media is the best way for you to stay in touch with them. As you interact with your followers, you can get specific insight into who they are and what they are interested in. This is crucial when it comes to tailoring your style to suit their needs.

Fiction writers love to interact with their readers. In doing so, they can gain an understanding about readers' interests, expectations, and demands. Believe it or not, your readers will demand certain things from you. In some cases, these demands surrounding events or characters. In others, your readers may ask you to write about specific topics. This is especially true in the non-fiction domain.

Another great way that writers leverage social media is to ask their readers to suggest topics they would like to read about. This is a great way of giving people what they want. Many times, readers have specific questions they would like you to answer for them. If you can provide those answers, your readers will surely follow you. So, do take the time to interact with your readers on social media whenever possible.

Capitalizing on Trends

Every now and then, events occur that capture news headlines and most people's attention. These events permeate the social landscape for any given length of time. These are wonderful opportunities for you to write on issues most people are interested in.

When you look to capitalize on trends, you need to pick a position and run with it. For example, let's assume you're looking to write on a current political issue. You may choose to remain neutral and just inform on the matter. That's perfectly fine. However, you must ensure that you always remain neutral. On the other hand, you might choose to state your position and write from that perspective. Therefore, your writing would have to be geared toward those folks who subscribe to your specific position. That means using the type of language and tone that is consistent with those folks.

Also, you must consider the overall profile of your readers. For instance, if you're address trends more popular with younger audiences, then you need to keep and light, fast-paced approach. Please bear in mind that younger individuals may not have the luxury of sitting down to read a long article. By the same token, your work might be oriented toward older individuals. These folks may have more time to devote to reading. Therefore, you can afford to make your point more elaborately.

Please keep in mind that any time you address current events, you must try to stay on the cutting edge. Thus, it's crucial for you to ensure that you present information that's consistent with your readers' wishes and desires. Ultimately, the topic itself doesn't really matter. What does matter is the way that you present it to your audience?

Important Considerations

Whenever you set out to write, it's always a good idea to put yourself in your readers' position. After all, you need to produce content that people would actually like to read. Often, this means putting yourself on the other side of the ball. Always ask yourself, "why would anyone read this?" The answer to this question can serve as a means of producing relevant content.

It's important to learn from mistakes. If previous content wasn't successful, you need to figure out why it didn't take off. That analysis will enable you to make changes so that your readers can get what they expect. Ultimately, it's about meeting your readers' expectations consistently so that you can continue to gain momentum in your following.

Lastly, please keep in mind that your readers change over time. With changing trends and situations, you might find that a winning combination may need to be altered. Therefore, it's always a good idea to stay in touch with your audience. That way, you can find out what they need and how you can deliver it to them. This is why staying in touch with readers is always a great idea. Successful writers build email lists. Then, they encourage their readers to submit questions and any suggestions. In doing so, you can ensure a constant feedback loop that allows you to find a great way of discovering new topics to keep you relevant.

Please bear in mind that successful writers always deliver what their readers want. That's the bottom line. If you can do that, you will always have a winning combination regardless of the topic itself. In the end, you will engage your readers in such a way that your communication will only continue to get stronger.

Chapter 4: Step 4 - Outlining Chapters Effectively

Proper organization is critical when it comes to writing a great book. Many times, novice writers commit a huge mistake by not properly organizing their content. Organizing content is all about ensuring that you have an adequate pace and flow to the way the material is presented. In other words, you have an appropriate setup, thereby ensuring your readers will have no trouble following your lead.

The entire organization process begins with outlining chapters based on the amount of information you wish to cover. Naturally, larger books with more content will need more chapters than books with less content. As a result, you need to be aware of how many sections you need to break your book down into.

In this chapter, we are going to take a look at how you can organize your content effectively while ensuring the overall flow of the material.

Understanding the Scope of Your Project

The single most important thing you need to consider when starting your project is its scope. By "scope," we mean the amount of material that you wish to cover. For example, if you're looking to cover a good chunk of material, then you are looking at a broader scope. If you're looking to cover less content, then you are looking at a narrower scope.

Please bear in mind that it's quite easy to get sucked into pushing for a broader scope. This can happen if you're not disciplined enough to write up an outline and then stick to it. This generally occurs when writers don't have a clear sense of where they are going. This is why you must ensure that you have a clear idea of where you want your project to go.

Consider this situation:

You are writing a book on holiday decorations. At first, you wish to focus solely on Christmas decorations. Then, you realize that Halloween decorations are also fun to do. So, you add those to the book. After that, you figure that Easter decorations would also be good. And so, you keep adding to the book.

Now, there is nothing wrong with the amount of information you plan to include in your book. The problem is that you never had a clearly defined scope. As such, your book appears to be a collection of random items all mashed together. Perhaps a better approach would have been to create separate volumes. For instance, one volume would focus solely on Christmas decorations, then the second on Halloween, the third on Easter, and so on.

In this example, you will find that simply adding and adding to your book will create a mix of ideas that may not necessarily fit well together once joined. So, do make sure that you have the right scope in mind when setting out to write your book.

Outlining Chapters

Once you have determined your scope, that is how much you plan to cover, you can move on to breaking down your content into chapters. A chapter is essentially a very broad idea that you will develop. In this development, you can break down the idea into as much detail as possible given the constraints you have. These constraints are limited to time and space. As for time, you might be on a deadline. As such, writing too much can negatively affect the time you have to complete the project. The second constraint is space. For instance, you may be working with a specific number of words. Therefore, you can't afford to ramble on too much. Otherwise, you'll run out of words.

To outline your chapters, all you need to do is break down your topic into subtopics. Each subtopic represents the main idea about the topic. These main ideas are important pieces that must be put together in order to assemble the entire puzzle.

There are no specific rules or guidelines on how many chapters should be in a book or the specific word count. This decision is based on your expertise and experience as a writer. A good rule of thumb is to break your main topic into about three to five main ideas. From there, you can use them to plan each chapter.

Now that you have your chapters outlined, then you can go on to decide the actual content that will be included in the chapter. This is largely a tactical decision, meaning that you'll choose what to include and what not, once you're in the writing process. For instance, many writers choose to leave out specific content that isn't directly related to their overall idea. Others choose to add content that they have not thought of before.

Please bear in mind that this organization is not set in stone. However, you must try your best to stick to your original plan as much as possible. That way, you can reduce the amount of wasted time spent on a topic.

How to Determine What Stays and What Goes

As mentioned earlier, the actual words you write in each chapter are a game-time decision. Some writers like to be very detailed. As such, they outline everything that will be included in the chapter. Others are less proactive. So, they don't actually plan out everything that will go into the chapter. They just sit down and write. It should be noted that you can get away with this when you're an experienced writer. If you're not that experienced in the topic itself, you can use other books on a similar subject as a starting point.

As you write, you may find that some ideas don't mesh well with the topic or other chapters in the book. So, you may choose to eliminate it from the book. Additionally, you may choose to deviate from your plan. This means that your instincts and knowledge will help you determine what to keep and what not.

Once you are satisfied with the direction a chapter has taken, you can review it to ensure it represents your idea. If needed, changes can improve the chapter. Otherwise, leaving the chapter as is, will help you move on. The aim is to progress as much as possible.

Figuring Out Your Word Count

This is one of the most common questions novice writers encounter. Determining the word count for a book is not always easy. However, there are parameters that you can follow. For example, a 5,000-word book is like a quick guide. At first, 5,000 might sound like a lot, but the reality is that it is not.

Additionally, a 10,000-word book is suitable for an introduction to a topic. Books ranging from 10,000 to 20,000 words offer a good level of detail into a specific topic. Books with a 20,000-to-30,000-word count are rather complex books. They generally require more content given their word count. Anything above 30,000 words is a voluminous book. At this level, you may have to really broaden your scope, or break down the topic into a very high level of detail. In the end, this level of detail will enable you to take up space you need to fully discuss the outcome.

Another good way of figuring out your word count is by looking at other similar books on the same topic. The size of the book can give you an adequate indication of how many words you might need to cover your ideas.

Sketching your Outline

Now that you have your chapters and content figured out, it's time to draft up your outline. Having an outline is essential to writing a book as soon as possible, and as accurately as possible. While it's true the some of the best writers are poor organizers, the fact is that you can't afford to be sloppy. As you gain more experience, you might be able to get past this limitation. However, novice writers would do well to write their outline.

A simple organization scheme can be using numerals for chapter numbers and bullet points for the subtopics. Then, you can consult your outline as you progress through the content. This is an important point as having a clear path for your book will lead you to successfully complete it.

Consider this sample outline:

1. Chapter 1: Introduction to the Stock Market
    a. Definition of the stock market
    b. Types of markets
    c. Products traded on the stock market
    d. People involved in the stock market

In this sample outline, we defined one chapter with four subtopics. The next step is to figure out the word count. You can do this by determining how much detail you wish to provide. If you aim to provide only general ideas, then 1,000 words might be enough for this chapter. However, if you want to really dig deep into the subject, you might find that 2,000 to 3,000 words might be more than enough.

You can follow this same system for all chapters in your book. In the end, you'll have a neatly polished outline for your book. It is often said that with a good outline, a book writes itself. This is true because having a good outline eliminates guesswork. As such, all you have to worry about is writing down the information you wish to communicate.

So, please take the time to think about how much content you wish to cover and how you intend to break it down. Doing this will save you time and headaches further down the road.

Chapter 5: Step 5 - Establishing Credibility Through Research

In the non-fiction world, credibility is crucial. After all, you cannot expect to be taken seriously if you're not careful with the information you put forth. Often, publishers and writers make sensationalist claims just to sell more books. However, these claims, if unfounded, can land you in serious trouble. Nevermind that your books won't sell, you can get sued. Therefore, it is important to conduct research effectively. That way, you can use these sources to back up any claims that you make as part of your publications.

When conducting research, it's a good idea to use the best practices implemented by academic writers. In academic writing, virtually everything you say must be backed up by some kind of credible source. This is why becoming familiar with research sites and other mainstream publications is a must. Moreover, you cannot expect to be taken seriously if you cite sources from non-credible sources. These sources include private individuals not considered experts, fringe organizations, or any other type of non-respected source.

In this chapter, we are going to take a look at how you can use research and trusted sources to boost your publications' credibility.

Not All Sources Are Created Equal

When looking at sources, it's often a question of common sense. For starters, there are organizations and institutions which are widely respected. For example, universities, international institutions, and official government organizations are all sources you can rely on. By citing information from these sources, you can back up the claims that you make in your works.

Perhaps the hardest part of conducting research is gaining access to these sources. This can be a challenge if you don't know where to look. So, let's take a look at the places where you can find the information you need.

- *Google Scholar.* This is the first stop for anyone looking to find credible sources on virtually any type of content. Google Scholar is a search engine that is dedicated specifically to finding academic articles published in major magazines and journals, while also offering books and articles.
- *Academic databases.* There are specific academic databases that are widely used by researchers. The best example of these is JSTOR. You can find a plethora of information there. However, please note that you may have to purchase a subscription to these databases if you want to have unlimited access.
- *Journals.* Most major fields of research have dedicated journals. These journals publish articles on topics related to

these fields of research. Since the vast majority of these journals are peer-reviewed, the publications in them are considered to be trustworthy. So, always search for journals on your chosen topic. Most back issues are freely available though you may have to purchase current editions.

- ***Subject matter experts***. A subject matter expert is a respected individual who is recognized for their expertise in a given area. Citing them is a great way of making your points come alive. You can cite interviews, articles, and lectures given by these individuals. So, always check out who the relevant experts are in your specific subject.

- ***Institutional information***. This type of information is generally posted by governments, international organizations, or private companies. Therefore, the information officially published by these institutions constitutes a real position you can use to back up your claims. For example, the United Nations publishes official positions on any number of subjects. As such, you can confidently use the United Nations as backing for the information you present.

Please bear in mind that virtually all of this information is freely available. So, all you have to do is take the time to do the research. While going to your local library still works well, you will find that using the power of the internet makes the research a lot faster and easier.

Using Disclaimers

Many writers use disclaimers as a means of warning readers that they are only publishing opinions and not making official recommendations. This is important, especially when you're not licensed to advise on a specific matter. For example, you can write a well-researched book on a health issue. However, if you're not a licensed practitioner in that field, you can get sued for the use readers make of that information. So, it's a good idea to include a disclaimer in which you free yourself of such responsibility.

Also, writers and publishers use disclaimers to make it known that the information they provide is for "entertainment purposes" only. Again, this type of disclaimer is widely used in areas that may constitute a risk for the publisher. So, it's always best to double-check if you need to include such disclaimers. A good rule of thumb is to include one whether you need it or not.

That being said, having a well-researched book will help you avoid being criticized for providing senseless information. As such, you can encourage readers to check out the sources you have presented. In that way, readers can take your analysis plus sources to derive their own conclusions.

Making Citations

Another important element to presenting your research is the use of citations. Depending on the nature of your publication, you can use simple citations such as, "according to…" or "in the opinion of…" These citations are used to introduce the source from which you have derived your information. Moreover, they are used in-text to inform the reader about where the information is coming from.

If you choose, you can use a specific citation format such as MLA, APA, or Vancouver. These types of citation methods are dependent on the type of content. For instance, MLA is used in most academic areas of research. Its defining characteristic is the use of footnotes at the bottom of the page. The APA format is the most used and can be implemented for any type of publication. The Vancouver citation method is mostly used within the medical sciences. Nevertheless, you can choose to use this format if it works best for you.

Ultimately, it's important to use a specific citation format, especially if you're looking to present a more academic paper. Most non-fiction books don't need such a level of detail. Nevertheless, it's always a good idea to put your best foot forward. This level of detail is used by professionals who are looking to position themselves as subject matter experts in their respective fields.

Being Careful with Plagiarism

Plagiarism is a sure-fire way of getting you banished from the face of the Earth. For instance, Amazon has very strict guidelines about how much duplicate content you can use. Generally speaking, you cannot upload a book that has more than 5% duplicate content. Therefore, a copy and paste approach is not going to cut it. While other platforms may let this slide, there is a very good chance you'll get called out on it eventually.

Plagiarism is considered fraud. While it may not get you in jail, it will automatically get you discredited. Once you are officially discredited, getting back into the good graces of readers is practically impossible. Therefore, you must be very careful about what information you use, and how you use it.

This is why the best way to go is to cite information that you use while limiting the use of direct quotes. Often, writers like to quote other speakers and writers directly. However, this may get you a strike for duplicate content. So, it's best to use direct quotes sparingly.

The best way to use information and quotes from other speakers and writers is to paraphrase. Paraphrasing means writing someone else's words in your own. For example, something like "in the words of Mark Twain…" can be a useful way of ensuring that you present the information you want without getting nailed for improper use.

Please bear in mind that plagiarism is the absolute worst thing you can do in the non-fiction world. So, it's best to ensure that you have the proper citations and give credit when it's due.

Working Around Plagiarism

Some unscrupulous folks simply rewrite other established materials. While this is perfectly legal, it's considered unethical. This is especially important if you're serious about positioning yourself within your respective field. There is nothing wrong with paraphrasing other stuff. Just make sure you follow proper citation guidelines.

Now, let's assume that you simply rewrite other material and publish under a pen name. That will do the trick. However, you will quickly find that most readers will catch on to your scheme. So, they may end up punishing you by leaving negative comments and bad reviews. Please keep in mind that bad comments are just as bad as being exposed to academic fraud. As such, ensuring that you always produce the best possible material is a must.

Lastly, please ensure that other writers you work with are on the same page as you are. While you will surely adhere to proper guidelines, you may not be so sure about others. If you suspect that other writers are fudging the rules, please make sure to call them out on it. If you fail to do so, your reputation may get tainted through no fault of your own.

Chapter 6: Step 6 - Understanding Subgenre

Genre is often at the center of discussion regarding successful non-fiction writing. Mainly, the discussion centers on getting the genre right. While that may seem relatively obvious, it isn't quite as straightforward as you might think. Defining a genre can be tough, especially if you're new to writing.

To define your book's genre, you must be first clear about what you're going to write. This is a crucial first step in determining your book's genre. Next, you need to have a clear vision of your book's scope. From there, you can safely determine your genre. Of course, that is easier said than done.

So, let's take a look at how you can define your book's genre and subgenre accurately. Best of all, you'll find that it's much easier than you think.

What Is Genre?

In essence, genre refers to the main topic of a book. This implies that you must have a clear sense of what your book is about. Now, in this book, we're dealing with one main, overarching genre which is non-fiction. As such, your book would most likely fall under the non-fiction genre.

While that's a great start, it's worth noting that such a description is too broad. Therefore, we must dig a little deeper and refine your book's genre and subgenre.

It's also important to note that genre encompasses rather extensive topics. These topics may cover a lot of different aspects. Yet, these are the main topics that readers will look for. From there, they may narrow down their search. This is why first appealing to a broad audience is key. From there, you can narrow your book's focus.

Please bear in mind that your book's genre should be reflected in its title. After all, your book's title will lead readers to find your content. So, you must make sure to include all the relevant words in the title. It will just make it easier for readers to find your work.

What Is Subgenre?

A subgenre is a narrower breakdown of your book's topic. In essence, it is the result of further refining your content. When you refine your content further down, you can come up with some rather specific topics to cover. As a result, you must ensure that your overall topic encompasses a clear subgenre.

Main topics such as knitting, gardening, personal finance, or home decoration are all too broad. Therefore, you must narrow your book's focus down to a clear perspective. This is why understanding your book's scope is so important. When you have a clear scope, then it's feasible for you to really drill down on the content you wish to cover.

Please keep in mind that the biggest mistake most novice writers make is leaving their scope too broad. Therefore, they have a tough time focusing on what they really want to say. If anything, they may find themselves bouncing all over the place. When that happens, there is no telling where the book may end up. This is why many writers begin working on a book, but never finish it.

Reflecting Genre and Subgenre in Your Book's Title

When selecting your book title, you must ensure that your genre and subgenres are adequately portrayed. In that regard, it can make an enormous difference between having a successful publication and a subpar one.

Consider this situation:

You have just completed a book on living room design. So, you choose to title it, "The Ultimate Living Room." This title is good, but it's a little too vague. Yes, you're reflecting on the fact that the book is about a living room. However, it doesn't tell the reader much more than that. Therefore, the book title doesn't make much sense.

In this case, a better title would be, "The Ultimate Living Room: 25 Great Decoration Ideas for a Small Budget." This title, while longer, encompasses everything you are looking to explain in this book. As such, any reader that comes across your book will know exactly what to expect. Consequently, this book title is much more effective when compared to the first one.

Please keep in mind that your clear understanding of your genre and subgenre must be stated in the title. Given the fact that there is a number of books on any number of topics, you need to make sure that yours stands out as much as possible. The best way to do this is by being absolutely clear about your genre in the title.

Improving Searchability

When you have a clearly defined genre, subgenre, and title, you drastically improve searchability. This is key regardless of the platform on which you sell your books. For example, if you sell your books on Amazon Kindle, readers search for topics based on keywords. These keywords are representative of the topic they are looking to read about. As such, you need to make sure that you have the right type of context in mind.

Now, the use of keywords is always important when looking to boost your book's marketing and sales. Keywords must therefore be used within the title. In the previous example, we were clear about including the terms "living room," "decoration," and "ideas."

Why?

Think about it for a minute.

Chances are that a reader would search for a book on this topic under the terms "living decoration ideas." In that case, you would have a clearly defined search. If your title represents these search terms, then you have automatically improved your book's chances of being discovered.

This is also true if you're selling your materials on your website. Your title can be discovered by Google. Therefore, it must reflect your genre and subgenre appropriately. This, in turn, will give search engines the opportunity to find your content amid tons of other types of content and materials.

Experienced writers know that visibility is paramount to successful content. By improving your searchability, you give your content a fighting chance to stand out. What searchability does is give your content a chance to shine through. Therefore, you have the opportunity to become successful based on your merits. Otherwise, great content may get lost in the shuffle. Needless to say, that is the last thing you want.

Thinking Big

When you have a clear idea of your genre, you can potentially break it up into an endless number of subgenres. This is important when looking at the bigger picture. The reason for this is based on the fact that you can create an entire series of books based on a general topic. From there, any number of specific subgenres can help you provide all types of readers options to choose from.

Let's consider this example.

You plan to write a series of books and sales and market. Since this is a broad topic, there are potentially endless types of books you could write. So, your job now becomes too narrow things down. For example, you could write a five-part series focused on sales and marketing for small businesses, startups, solopreneurs, online businesses, and family companies.

In this example, you took a broad topic, sales, and marketing, and then broke it down into five more specific topics. In the end, you were able to make the topic work effectively by creating a series of books. Now, instead of having one large volume divided into five parts, you have five separate volumes.

What's the advantage here?

The advantage is that you can boost your sales by appealing to a broader customer base, offering more selections, and focusing on specific market niches. For instance, a person who is interested in sales and market for small businesses would be interested in purchasing the volume dedicated to that topic. In contrast, if you had one volume with five topics, that interested reader may pass as your book contains topics they are not interested in.

Do you see how powerful this approach can be?

Ultimately, your goal is to leverage your writing skills so you can produce a greater income. In the end, you can do that with the same amount of effort. The only difference is that you are using your talents in a much more productive way.

Please keep in mind that you need to have a pretty good idea as to the genre and subgenre of your content even before you write a single word. While it is certainly possible that things can change along the way, it's also important to keep in mind that having a clear starting point can make the difference between a successful book and a disappointing one.

There is no question that you have what it takes to produce highly successful content. So, it's a question of focusing it appropriately. In that case, it will make your job that much easier. That's why it's important to give yourself a hand. Rather than make things harder than they have to be, you can improve your chances right from the start. So, make sure you have a clearly defined genre, subgenre, and title. When you put them all together, you'll have a recipe for a successful book or even a series of books.

Chapter 7: Step 7 - Building a Winning Formula

At this point, we have laid out the groundwork needed to build a winning formula. This winning formula is about developing a system that can help you become the most successful writer that you can.

Now, it's important to note that this isn't a magic formula. As such, this isn't something you can pull out of a box and let it roll. This winning formula is a highly personalized one. This means that you need to develop a keen understanding of the various elements discussed in this guide. From there, you can create a system that will help you deliver successful content time and time again.

So, we are going to dedicate this chapter to bringing everything together so that you can build a personal winning formula. From there, you will discover just how effective writing can truly be.

Playing to Your Strengths

This is pivotal. All writers have personal wheelhouse. That means there are topics and content that they are much better at than others. Therefore, play to your strengths, especially in the early going.

As you make a name for yourself, you want to put your best foot forward. As such, playing to your strengths makes perfect sense. For example, if you're a finance expert, then go down that path. Sure, it might be really exciting to think about writing the next great novel. However, the idea here is to build momentum. By building your momentum, you build your self-confidence. That is what gives you the ability to branch outside your comfort zone.

Also, please keep in mind that readers want value as much as possible. So, using your area of expertise to its fullest potential makes sense. Doing so will put you in a position of strength. In contrast, branching out into other areas may put you in a tough spot. So, playing to your strengths is always the best approach.

With time, you can venture outside the box. You can try working on other topics that you have always wanted to. By then, you'll already have a strong foundation beneath you. Consequently, you'll have the confidence to help you put your best foot forward. As a writer, your experience will help you figure out what works and what doesn't.

So, don't be afraid to go on the power play early on. Eventually, you'll have the experience you need to try new things out.

Use Your Voice

Throughout this guide, we've talked about being yourself. This is so true, especially when you're playing to your strengths. Using your voice is crucial when it comes to building rapport with your readers. Believe it or not, readers can pick up when you're trying to be someone you're not. Readers can tell by the way the words flow or don't.

You see, writing is a skill that is honed over time. It's part of an author's thought process. So, the challenge in writing is to organize your thought process in such a way that it's logical and coherent. That will lead readers down a path they can fully comprehend.

It's also important to keep in mind that inexperienced writers tend to produce well-written, but disjointed and incoherent text. Therefore, the challenge becomes to articulate your ideas clearly.

How can you articulate your arguments?

Use your outline!

Yes, when you use your outline, you can produce high-quality content that can lead you to focus your thoughts clearly and coherently. An outline helps you narrow your scope while keeping you on track. Otherwise, you run the risk of simply ranting on about personal experiences or things you know about. While this is useful to a certain degree, all successful books need to have a clear narrative.

Of course, you might hear some writers saying that sticking to outlines can be highly restrictive. That is true to some extent. It requires a lot of experience to simply write without any kind of formal outline, concept, and objective. As you gain experience, it's always a good idea to have a clearly defined concept.

One other thing. Please avoid trying to do everything in your head. When you try to do everything in your head, thoughts can often get muddled and confused. This can lead you to get stuck at any point in your book. So, make sure you write everything down. While it is totally possible to make changes, keeping a written record helps you establish the path you wish to take your readers on. Think of it as building a roadmap before setting out on your journey.

Stick to a Specific Narrative

There are some truly gifted writers out there. They can produce quality content on a number of topics. They can write about practically anything. That's both blessing and a curse.

You see, writers often become known for a specific type of genre. Think about all of the great fiction writers. They end up getting typecast into a specific genre because they are successful in it. As such, they focus their energy on that genre. After a while, they don't venture out into other genres, not because they don't have the talent, but to avoid confusing readers.

For instance, let's assume you have made a name for yourself in the medical field. People know you as a great health care professional. Naturally, people would be happy to see you produce content on health and wellness. Over time, you gain quite a bit of traction in this field. Then, you realize your lifelong dream of writing a novel. However, your readers are confused. You're known as a great healthcare professional. So, why are you writing a novel?

Do you see the point in this argument?

Now, it should be noted that lots of folks decide to make a 180-degree turn and write a novel. Also, some folks choose to write about topics they love. That's all well and good. The point is to choose a topic and run with it. Who knows, this could truly put you on the map.

Once you make a name for yourself, you must then commit to that genre. That way, your popularity, and success can just compound with each piece of content you publish. Eventually, you'll have the right following around you.

Branching Out into Other Genres

So, what if you can write about other genres?

In that case, it's best to go with a pen name. This is what all great writers do. You see, once a writer becomes known for a specific genre, they have no choice but to go with it. That's why adopting a pen name makes sense.

By taking on another personality, you can ensure that readers will not be biased by your previous success. In fact, some readers may be skeptical about your ability to be successful in other topics. Therefore, using a pen name can remove that bias from your readers' minds.

There is one significant upside to using a pen name. If for some reason, your content flops, your usual reputation won't take a hit. In a way, this takes the pressure off writing new content. For instance, if your first novel flops, you can simply learn from the mistakes. As such, it won't count against your current standing with your followers. This is one of the biggest advantages that writing offers good authors.

The downside to this is that you'll be practically starting from scratch. Your new persona won't have any kind of following. Therefore, you'll need to put in the time and effort to properly market your new content. Nevertheless, your previous experience can help you market your new content effectively.

As your new genre gains momentum, please keep in mind that you may need to eventually come out as the genius behind the magic. Nevertheless, you won't have to worry too much about that. Since your new content has gained popularity, readers will be impressed, not confused.

How Much Should You Write?

This question gets asked all the time. Many novice writers don't know how much they should write. Also, new authors don't have a sense of how often they should publish new material.

Well, there is a short and long answer to that question.

The short answer is that you should publish new material whenever you have it ready. This means that if it takes you six months to write a new book, then publish it then. Additionally, if it takes you two years to write one, then your audience will have to wait for you that long. Of course, you shouldn't take decades to come up with new material.

The long answer is that you should publish material when it's prudent to do so. For example, let's say that you published a highly successful book three months ago. Since you are a prolific author, you already have two more books in the final editing phase. So, you plan to publish as soon as the next one is ready.

That can be a mistake.

Why?

You see, successful authors publish new content until the sales of the previous ones have stalled. When sales stall, it means that everyone who wanted to read your book has already done it. So, it's time for something new.

Other writers like to follow a specific tempo. For instance, they publish a new book every six months, or once a year. If this sounds like you, it could be a good approach. After all, if your readers get used to your writing tempo, you may find yourself building a steady income stream.

In the end, your winning formula is about building a system that works for you based on good practices. You will find out what works for you soon enough. So, take the time to discover what works for you. Sometimes, you simply have to learn from your mistakes. However, the result will be totally worth it!

Conclusion

Thank you very much for taking the time to complete this guide. We hope that you now have a great sense of how to write non-fiction content. At this point, you should be able to understand how you wish to pursue your writing endeavors. Mainly, it's about ensuring that you have a system that can lead you to become a successful writer.

So, please take the time to go over any of the concepts provided in this guide. Repetition is a very important part of learning. As such, reviewing previous lessons is always a great way of ensuring that your knowledge has been fixated in your mind. Moreover, review and practice will help you become the best writer you can possibly be.

Often, developing great skills is a question of time. While we would all love to magically flip a switch, the fact is that most of the skills we learn in life come as the result of years of work and practice. Please keep the 10,000-hour rule in mind. This rule states that we need about 10,000 hours of practice before we can truly master a skill.

Now, does that mean that it will take you 10,000 hours to become a great writer?

Not necessarily.

What this idea means is that you need to put in the time and effort to become a successful writer. The more time and practice you put into your writing endeavors, the better you will get. Naturally, this approach means that your success is proportional to the amount of work and sacrifice you are willing to put in.

Please take this opportunity to truly allow your efforts to shine through. You already have the most important elements you need to be successful. So, it is just a matter of making your efforts become a testament to the hard work you are prepared to invest in. The difference between mediocre writers and great ones is the amount of effort and dedication put into their craft. The best writers in history were able to combine hard work and natural talent. Ultimately, this combination has led to some of the most famous works.

Good luck and happy writing!

Book 3: How to Edit Writing

7 Easy Steps to Master Writing Editing, Proofreading, Copy Editing, Spelling, Grammar & Punctuation

Jaiden Pemton

Introduction

When it comes to editing, it is crucial to take your time and be thorough, give attention to the seemingly minor details, and interact with the material on a deeper level to ensure the purpose is being fulfilled. No matter which industry you're working with in the writing world, editing is a universal requirement. Whether you're editing your own writing or serving as an editor for another writer, this guide will show you the top-notch editing strategies, which will be sure to set the content you edit apart in your industry and yield ultimate success as an editor.

It is not possible to predict exactly how many drafts you will need to generate before a piece of writing is ready to go out into the world. Ultimately, the more thorough you are, the fewer drafts you will need to generate. The task of editing requires deep focus and willingness to engage with the content wholly to catch the smallest mistakes, inconsistencies, or areas where the text's purpose is getting lost. Whether you are editing your own writing or someone else's, it is crucial to develop skills that set you apart and help you achieve the most accurate and efficient editing strategy.

When it comes to editing, it is easy to fall into the trap of getting bored or exhausted by the content and skimming over important details. You may reach a point where you have looked over the same words so often. You struggle to determine the right word to use when something doesn't sound right or figuring out how to re-instate the purpose.

You may find yourself feeling so eager to have the content wrapped up and turned in that you start missing small details, which can be a vital mistake. As the editor, it is your job to get the piece of writing that is as close to perfection as possible. If your text is full of errors you did not catch in the editing stage, it will push readers away. This guide will provide you with ideas for maintaining your own energy and enthusiasm throughout the editing process and utilizing tactics such as giving the writing space and editing in reverse to keep a fresh perspective.

In this guide you will find a comprehensive step-by-step reference format with everything you need to know about the editing process. You will be provided with in-depth knowledge of the stages of editing, the importance of reading work aloud, how to manage the small formatting details, how to deeply interact with the content to ensure the message is getting across, and creative strategies you can implement to look at the content differently. Additionally, the guide contains excellent tips for keeping your editing process lively and engaged the whole way through.

The chapters of this guide will take you through each step of the editing journey to help you avoid common mistakes and develop your own thorough process. Each chapter is designed with astounding detail to help you stay on track and address any questions or concerns you have along the way.

Chapters are subtitled and easy-to-follow with examples of tips, tricks, techniques, and things to avoid. Regardless of if you are editing your own writing or someone else's, this guide has all the tools you need to set yourself apart as an expert editor and is sure to serve as the perfect guide to revolutionize your editing experience.

Happy writing!

Chapter 1: Step 1 - Breaking Editing into Stages

As an editor, your role is to make sure everything is clear to the reader. If the reader struggles to read the text, either because it is swaying from the purpose or there are too many mistakes with formatting or grammar, they will have a much harder time reaching the end of the piece. Your job is to advocate for the reader by making their journey through the text as easy as possible and ensuring that they are impacted by the text when they reach the end. To increase levels of clarity and consistency for the reader, you must be persistent in the correction and improvement process. Your role as the editor includes correcting the structure, style, grammar, spelling, punctuation, point of view, and information order. Before you begin, it is vital to familiarize yourself with the client's guidelines (if you are editing for another writer) or the publisher.

Breaking Down the Stages

The editing process includes several stages. The first stage is structural or developmental editing, in which you complete a rough copy edit. Line editing and copy editing are the second stages of the process, and the rough copy edit is the result of this stage. The final step is the fine or final copy edit, which involves final proofreading and preparing for the graphic design and "final proof" stages, which will occur right before publication.

In some cases, if the writer has already done a great deal of initial self-editing on the piece, the structural stage may not be necessary, as the work is already structurally sound. If you are writing and editing your own piece, you will need to make plans to send it on to a professional editor to ensure the work is structurally sound, and then again for the final proofreading. This is because, at some point, you will have been looking at your content so much that you will not be able to target any other edits that need to be made.

Stage 1: Structural Editing

The role of the structural editor is to review the writing from a broader standpoint. The structural stage is not meticulously examining the details but instead considering the text's more significant picture issues. This editor needs to be aware of who the target audience is and the author's primary goal. Editors of fiction stories need to ensure that the plot, dialogue, character, and point of view are clearly expressed and follow the same structure. Editors of nonfiction should examination the general organization of the content and question it for clarity and consistency of the argument and supporting evidence.

Scheduling Structuring Consultations

Suppose the structural editor is not the writer of the manuscript. In that case, they will need to consult with the author to discuss the main idea the author is trying to express so they can evaluate it for clarity. Additionally, the author and structural editor should confirm the style manual that is expected in editing. They should be on the same page regarding the style which will be used, which can be defined in a style sheet. The style sheet is a tool for the structural editor to refer back to throughout the editing process, including all necessary rules regarding punctuation, fonts, headings, capitalization, etc.

Once the editor has come up with a list of structural edits, they will need to meet with the author again to discuss the structural improvements and why they are suggesting them. The structural editor may find that the manuscript is structurally sound and does not need many modifications and, therefore, may advise the author to proceed to the copyediting stage.

Determining the Authority of the Structural Editor

In some cases, the structural editor and the author may agree that the structural editor has full flexibility with their changes, including length, word count, number of chapters, or even the point of view. However, in other cases, the structural editor may be expected to consult with the author to receive approval before making any corrections. Another option is for the structural editor to make all corrections as suggestions in a separate draft and submit it to the client so that all the edits made are visible and can be approved or declined.

Increasing Clarity and Consistency

The structural editor must keep in mind that their job is not to entirely change the manuscript but rather, to make it better. That said, they should move and delete sentences or paragraphs only when it is altogether necessary to increase clarity and consistency. The structural editor can make suggestions on switching the order of chapters, creating new chapter sections, adjusting the table of contents, or creating appendices, descriptions, or introductions.

Focusing on the Bigger Picture

Although the structural editor can correct grammar, spelling, and punctuation, this is not their primary focus. The manuscript will endure further stages of editing, which are more dedicated to these small details. The structural editor should maintain focus on the bigger picture. They should be asking themselves if the way the text is set up is easy to follow, if the theme is being clearly expressed throughout the manuscript etc. If the structural editor is different than the editors who will be working on the manuscript in its later stages, they may choose not to correct the finer details.

Stage 2: Line Editing

The first part of copy editing (the second stage of the editing process) is line editing. The line edit is sometimes called a "rough copy edit" and can only occur after the manuscript has been evaluated for structural soundness. The line editing process does not aim to correct every minor error but rather to continue building on the manuscript's consistency as a whole. The copy editor will check for ways to improve the tone and style to better match the manuscript's goals. If fact-checking needs to occur, the line editing phase is where that will happen. The line reader should fact check information such as places, links, events, and references provided in the manuscript to ensure that the statements are correct. If the manuscript needs an index, it will require a separate "editing pass," which can be done by an indexer or by the line editor.

Addressing Structural Inconsistencies

The role of the line editor is to catch any structural issues which may have been overlooked. If there are remaining structural errors, the manuscript may require further structural editing. The line editor must bear in mind the manual guide chosen for the document to ensure that all of the content is per this manual. The line editor will rely on the style sheet to ensure consistency and add to the style sheet. The style sheet serves as an outline for rules concerning punctuation, spelling, acronyms, capitalization, fonts, and heading and is crucial for creating dependability within the manuscript.

Catching Major Spelling, Punctuation, and Grammatical Errors

As the line editor proceeds through the editing process, they have the authority to make grammatical changes, move sentences and paragraphs around, select deletion of repetitive information, and suggest rewrites for sentences and paragraphs. Their goal is to catch the significant spelling and punctuation errors to improve the grammar of the manuscript.

Conducting Editing Passes

In many cases, the manuscript will pass through a variety of line editing stages. Each stage is considered an 'editing pass,' Each manuscript requires a different number of passes to ensure that all significant corrections have been made. The line editor's role does not extend to correcting minor errors; however, more minor errors may be encountered as the manuscript goes through more passes.

Creating the Final Copy Edit

The final stage of the copyediting process is the most meticulous of all. It is the final stage of corrections before the final design and proofreading stages before publication. If the writing will not be published, the 'final copy edit' is the final stage of the editing process. The stakes are high in this stage, and the process is more detailed.

When copyediting things like newsletters, applications, and reports, which are not going to be published, the copy editor can assume that the document has already undergone self-editing and should not address too many errors. The copy editor strives to catch the last remaining grammatical, punctuation, or spelling errors that were not detected during the initial editing stages.

In the case of a manuscript that will be published, it must receive a final copy edit before it is sent into the final stages of design and proofreading before publication. Manuscripts that need this last copy edit before the designing stage are fiction or nonfiction manuscripts, annual reports, or any other report that will be distributed publicly.

Checking the Manuscript with Fresh Eyes

The copy editor's role is to catch any basic editing that was missed in the line editing stage, using the style sheet and any other manual guides for reference on appropriate stylistic decisions. With fresh eyes, the copy editor will correct any minor mistakes that have not previously been addressed. They will check for any inconsistencies in the text and deal with information such as appendices, index, publication information, and the table of contents that have not been addressed by the line editor.

Preparing for the Final Stage

After the first copy editing pass occurs, the copy editor will work with the author to determine if it is sufficient or needs to go through another pass to ensure no errors. Before the document is turned in or passed on to the design stage, the copy editor must be able to confirm with confidence that there are no errors, and the document is fully ready for the following step.

Chapter 2: Step 2 - Reading Work Aloud

Have you ever been trying to edit an essay with a peer or teacher and been told to "Try reading it aloud?" This is a common editing strategy because it pulls us out of the space of skimming and forces us to engage with the text differently. The process of reading aloud can serve as a useful tool to catch the areas that seem "off" but can be easily ignored when reading the text in your head.

Reading aloud not only builds continuity and confidence with what has been written, but it also helps you to engage with the meaning differently, comprehend what is on the paper, identifying the writing voice, and establishing areas where the flow could be improved.

Significant Benefits of Reading Aloud

There are several significant benefits to reading aloud. The first is that the process of reading aloud helps you to hone in on dialogue and narrative, capture its real authenticity, and ensure that all the right characters are speaking at the right time to keep things flowing. Reading aloud is visual and helps paint a picture in your mind as you read the text, leading you to make changes or say more in some text regions to make these images more potent for the reader.

Reading aloud also yields a more remarkable ability for self-expression. If you are the writer and the editor of your own piece, reading aloud can help establish the connection between your speaking and writing voice. Additionally, reading aloud helps build on your internal listening skills, which can help you tune in to the writing voice of yourself (if you are editing your own work) or the writer you are working for. This can yield more significant success in future writings.

Editing for Clarity and Correctness

In terms of editing for clarity and correctness, reading aloud helps you to sound out words, catch stumbling blocks created by poor punctuation, detect the use of syllables, and catch misspellings. It is much easier to tell if a sentence is a run-on or a word is misspelled if you have the chance to verbalize it. Not only is reading aloud the best way to establish fluidity, build connections, and catch otherwise unnoticeable errors in the text you edit, it can also develop your skills in public speaking.

Reading Aloud as a First Step

When it comes to editing your writing, reading aloud is crucial in catching the mistakes that become easy to miss. As soon as you finish writing your piece, it's a good idea to read it aloud before doing anything else. This is an excellent tactic for catching some initial structural and grammatical errors right from the beginning, which will make the rest of the process much more comfortable. As you read the writing aloud, keep a pen or highlighter handy that you can use to mark areas where you notice yourself stumbling or feeling confused at what was just said.

Establishing Text Flow

When you read aloud, you can establish how your writing flows, how a particular section works (or doesn't work) with the next, and if you are staying in the active voice. One of the best ways to catch passivity is through the reading aloud process. If you find yourself stumbling or getting lost on the message of what you're reading, that is a clear sign that edits are needed.

As you read your work aloud, it becomes clearer whether or not the correct punctuation marks are being used. If you notice pauses, questions, or exclamations in your oral reading, there is reason to believe you should either insert a comma or add a period. If you find yourself going on and on in a single sentence, that's a good sign that sentence is a run-on and needs to be broken up. By listening to your pauses, you can better avoid punctuation errors and run-on sentences. The read-aloud also gives you a process to question your grammar and the meaning of the work. If you don't know what you're reading about, your other readers certainly will not.

Deepening Reader Understanding

To that same token, if you find yourself growing bored as you read, it's a good sign that a particular section needs to be cut.

Boredom while reading is usually a result of the momentum slowing down too much or the writing theme becoming lost to leave the reader asking, "What's going on here and what's the point?" If you feel like a specific section of the writing is slow or confusing, it should either be changed or cut out entirely.

Verbalizing as a Thinking Tool

Saying things out loud about your writing can also be helpful when it comes to remembering ideas for later. If you have an idea but can't write it down, speak it into existence. Listening to yourself talk about it can help form the idea into a memory that you can later take back to your writing desk. Similarly, as you come up with new ideas of things to write or elements to add to your pieces, talk the ideas through with yourself beforehand. It's a good idea to speak these ideas out loud, ask yourself questions the reader may ask, work through inconsistencies and unclear parts, and genuinely engage with the dialogue. In doing this, you can already bring an outside voice to your writing, which can help eliminate ideas that won't get you very far and encourage you to think more.

Personifying Dialogue

Because dialogue is a verbal exchange between multiple characters, the only way to truly measure its efficiency is by verbalizing it. One way to do this is by viewing the dialogue like that of a script. As you read, pay attention to how natural and authentic the dialogue sounds. Does it sound rigid or overly rehearsed? Is each line being spoken necessary? Is there more that needs to be said? Does the correct character talk about each line, or should someone else be saying it? To keep your readers engaged, you must establish this sense of engagement in yourself by reading aloud.

Making Pace Adjustments

Reading your work aloud helps with pacing as it gives you an idea of which parts of the writing are fast-pasted and engaging and where things slow down. Once you have this knowledge, you can question whether or not certain areas are moving too quickly and trying to tackle too much (which can leave the reader feeling confused and strung along) or if they are too slow (which can leave the reader feeling bored and uninspired).

Using your pen or highlighting tool, mark the areas where you notice significant differences in the pacing, and ask yourself if each scene is correctly paced or would be more potent if it was slowed down or sped up. Slowing things down can help the reader take a break from something hectic that just happened or build tension for something wild that is about to happen. Reading aloud is the only way to catch these pacing details.

Honing in on Important Details

Along with improving your pacing, reading aloud also serves to enhance the flow of the writing. As mentioned previously, it is easy for our brains to skip over the seemingly minute details to get to the point of what we are reading. This is especially true if you have been looking at the same piece of writing repeatedly. At some point, your subconscious begins to ignore the finer details. Eventually, even as you read aloud, you may find yourself trying to skip words or move things around. Make a note of these things and ask yourself if your natural desire to do this warrants some sort of change in the text.

Establishing Specific Areas to Edit

Hearing the work you have written read aloud often brings things to light that are hard to notice as our eyes repeatedly scan the page. In the early editing stages specifically, there is a lot more work to be done than we may realize. The writing may be too wordy, too fast, too slow, or lack emotion and passion, have inefficient dialogue, or simply lack interest level. If you are a writer who plans to send your manuscript to an editor to work with, be sure to read it aloud and sort through things first. This way, you can provide more input to your editor on what you need help with. If you are the editor of someone else's work, encourage them to read it aloud beforehand so they can provide more of a basis for discussion. Once it is in your hands, continue to read it aloud until everything sounds right.

Reading Aloud to Others

The final step of reading work aloud in the editing process is to read aloud to another person (or people). The person you read in front of can be anyone from a close friend, family member, or partner, to a peer or even a stranger. Regardless of who you choose to read aloud to, you can rely on the innate appreciation of social behavior to increase your desire to solve problems and pay more in-depth attention to the writing.

Reading aloud is typically a more vulnerable and intimidating experience, especially if you read something you wrote yourself. When we read material aloud, our natural social instincts become heightened because we know other people listen to us and draw opinions from what we say. We have an innate desire to perform well in front of others and receive positive feedback. Your responses will be heightened from this space of vulnerability and slight nervousness, and you may notice things you began to ignore in previous readings subconsciously. You will be extra sensitive to inconsistencies in pace, rhythm, and flow, as well as if a particular section drones on for too long. This heightened sensitivity will allow you to make even more changes and come closer to perfection than you could be reading only to yourself. In this state, you will also have a deeper appreciation for the writing structure, and your desire to produce a pleasing effect will increase.

The heightened sensitivity and social pressure of reading aloud to another person will make the errors in grammar, flow, and punctuation leap out even further, as you will feel nervous about making mistakes. You will be likely to look upon the writing with more meticulous eyes as you consider the fact that other listeners are drawing their conclusions and making their judgments. This will motivate you to solve the problems you encounter within the text as quickly and efficiently as possible.

Chapter 3: Step 3 - Setting Things Apart

When it comes to elements like headings, captions, indexes, appendixes, tables, and contents lists, it can be hard to stay focused. Writers tend to focus more on the main point of what they are trying to say, the characters they develop, and what they want the reader to take away. It is typical for the seemingly fewer essential elements of the writing to slip through the cracks. With the competition of the writing industry and the bustling state of the world, editors cannot afford to be careless with these elements.

Giving Readers Something to Skim

As people navigate their busy lives, they are more likely to skim through writing than profoundly engaging from start to finish. To capture the reader's attention, you must be concise and convincing, drawing them to slow down and engage more deeply with what is being said. When a customer is looking for a piece of content to contend with, they are not reading page after page of the writing itself. Instead, they are looking at the headings, captions, indexes, appendixes, tables, and contents lists to tell them more about what to expect and help them decide if it is worth their time. If a reader is confused by the headings and cannot figure out what will be said in each section, they will have no desire to read that section.

However, if they see even one or two headers that specifically pique their interest, they will be more likely to read on. Readers will be turned off by sloppy captions as well, whereas well-written captions will help them engage further with the content from the start.

Additionally, readers can become overwhelmed by overly detailed indexes or disengaged with overly brief indexes. Although these elements seem small, they serve as the signposts that allow the writer to communicate the purpose of the text, summarize, and highlight the key takeaways. That said, each of these elements is crucial for slowing a reader down in their tracks and drawing them into what the writer has to say. The engagement with these elements should compose at least half of the editing journey.

Tying up Loose Ends

As the editor (of your work or someone else's), it is your job to tie up loose ends and ensure the presented content is clear and well-supported. The hope of every editor of someone else's writing is that the writer will have done some of this work on their own first (for example, by reading aloud).

However, this is not always the case; as many times, the writer will have burnt out from the writing process and will feel that they cannot look at the text any longer. As the editor, you must be able to work with the content in hand, no matter what state it is in. In the cases of editors working for clients, this may look like doing the "dirty work" the writer did not have the energy to do—writing the copy for headings, captions, or any other missing elements. If you are both the writer and the editor, you must be able to enter into a new space in the editing process, in which you are prepared to take on this "dirty work" with a fresh mind.

Conducting Regular Check-ins

After you have checked for grammatical errors, punctuation errors, and spelling errors in the main text, it is good to check for the same things in things like the major headings and the names of people in the manuscript. This check-over should occur in both the manuscript and proofing stages, as errors can be missed even with several editing passes. The last thing you want to happen is to catch these errors once a piece of writing is already published, and the only way to avoid this is by being as meticulous as possible in the editing stages.

Writing Headings and Subheadings

Headings and subheadings must be consistent with pre-established formatting, and they should all look the same (same font, same size, same position, same general length). In general, these elements of all main headings such as chapter titles, 'Contents,' 'Preface,' 'Index,' and 'Appendix' should follow the same model. These headings should be organized logically, separating the text into easy-to-follow sections. Titles should usually have more space above than below them, with spacing varying slightly depending on the heading's importance (for example, a critical heading may be provided with more space, have a larger font sized, and be centered with more space than the average subheading).

Essential articles are marked by the most massive headlines, which should be placed near the top of the page to avoid imbalance. Another tip is to use short words in headings and subheadings as often as possible to avoid confusion that can arise from overusing hyphens.

Not only do headings and subheadings need to be correctly formatted and consistent with one another, but they also need to grab the reader's attention and make them want to read on. In many cases, the writing draft may have some headings in place by the time they reach the editing stage. However, just because the titles exist does not mean they are influential or will serve the purpose of drawing readers closer. Publications will be more successful if they have headers that make a clear statement, impress advertisers, and keep readers feeling hungry for more. If this job is not accomplished in the first drafts, it is the editor's job to rewrite the headers to make it so.

Writing and Editing Captions

When it comes to editing captions, you must remember that even if readers are not engaging deeply with the text's body, they will be naturally drawn to images and pieces of text set apart from the rest in caption form. Captions should be kept short and relevant and should be conclusive with what is happening in the illustration and the surrounding body text. Ideally, the reader will be able to understand what is happening on the page by merely examining a clear-cut caption. As the editor, you must be aware of any cross-references in the text which correspond to illustrations and make sure the figure numbers in the captions line up. It is best to use as few page numbers in cross-references as possible to save yourself the cost and the possibility of requiring further edits.

Dividing the Process into Stages

If you're feeling overwhelmed by the intensity of the editing process, don't worry. There are undoubtedly many things to consider, and the stakes are high for catching as many edits as possible to avoid misprints and ensure the publications' success. That said, there is an excellent technique for keeping yourself on track and preventing overwhelm in the editing stage. This technique involves splitting up each of these "smaller elements" of the writing and focusing on them one at a time. Start with the headings. Confer with your guidelines on which font style, size, and spacing to use in the titles and subheadings, and check them through for consistency. After you have gone over the headings several times, move on to captions. Once again, confer with the guidelines for caption writing.

With each caption, ask yourself if it is clear, concise, and in line with what is happening in the image and the rest of the text. After captions, move on to tables and content lists. Make sure the content lists direct readers to where they need to go to find specific information. As for the tables, make sure the information provided highlights the text's main points or provides the reader with necessary background information (like statistics of case studies).

Next, move on to the index and appendix. Check each one to ensure it contains just the right amount of detail, not too much, and not too little. By breaking up each of these steps and dedicating time to each, you are more likely to catch inconsistencies.

Chapter 4: Step 4 - Utilizing Isolation Strategies

As you move through the editing process, it may become gradually more difficult to tell one idea of the text from the next. After a while, words begin to meld together, and the overall context may become muddled. To keep a clear perspective with each text block, you need to be proactive with text isolation strategies. Later in the guide, we will explore further strategies for maintaining clarity, such as taking space from the text and reading in reverse. However, these strategies generally take place after the manuscript has undergone several editing passes. For this chapter, we will focus on methods of text isolation in the early stages of editing.

Keeping the Focus

Throughout the initial editing process, it can be helpful to use a blank sheet of paper to cover the text you have not yet reviewed. By doing this, you can keep your attention focused on the text at hand instead of looking ahead or becoming distracted. As you finish reading specific paragraphs, make a mark to show that you have looked at them, and don't go back until you are in the next full editing pass.

Breaking the Text into Sections

Another strategy of isolation goes hand-in-hand with the concept of taking space. Depending on your project's length, it is a good idea to establish how you will break up the text before beginning your editing process. It is very difficult to be thorough in the copyediting stages if you don't create small "cut off points" or benchmarks to keep you on track. If you are editing a poem of six stanzas with four lines in each stanza, it would be smart to give yourself about half an hour to work with the material.

Take about four minutes per stanza, with one minute dedicated to each line. You can use this minute to read the line aloud, isolated from all the rest of the poem, to check for flow and word choice. After you have finished all four lines of a particular stanza, take one minute to evaluate the stanza as a whole. Take a moment to breathe, then move on to the following stanza.

Considering Interest Level and Familiarity

On the other hand, if you are editing a 300-page book, the process of text isolation will look much different. You should begin by asking yourself how easy or challenging this particular content is for you to edit. Is it a topic you're familiar with, or is it entirely new knowledge that may take longer to process and could require additional research? Is it something that piques your interest, or is it out of your general interest area and could become tedious as you go along? Is the book written for young audiences and will be a quick and easy read, or is it designed to be intellectually challenging and maybe more time consuming to get through?

Knowing the answer to all of these questions ahead of time will make it much easier for you to understand how to divide the text into isolated sections. Not only will this allow you to be more thorough, but it will also make the process of editing much more manageable. Once you have determined the project's density and your interest level and familiarity, it's time to develop a system for breaking up the text.

Working Through Sections Quickly

If you are familiar with the content in the 300-page book and find it reasonably interesting, you will likely be able to work faster. In this case, you may choose to divide the 300-pages up into ten sections of ten pages, which you can read through fairly quickly. In between each area, take a brief break to look away from the text you just read, leaving it in the past as you move on to a new isolated piece of text. During this break, you may choose to be on your phone, use the restroom, or take a drink of water. Regardless of what you do, make sure to clear your head of the text you just read (besides the general context that you will need to take with you), and allow yourself to move on fully to the next piece.

Determining How Many Sections to Read Per Day

Once you've developed a general system of section-lengths and subsequent breaks, you can decide how many sections to read per day. If each section of ten pages takes fifteen minutes to read, you may choose to do the work in two days, putting in 1-2 hours of work per day. With each isolated section of the text, be sure to give yourself a few moments to reflect upon what you just read, and make notes of your questions and observations to refer back to on the following editing pass.

Working Through Dense Content

If the 300-page book is dense content that is harder for you to understand or feel interested in, you can expect that it will take more time, and you may also need longer breaks in between. You may decide, for example, to divide the readings up into ten-page sections but give yourself 30-40 minutes to complete them. After sitting down for this amount of time to edit a ten-page section, you may find yourself ready for a more extended break, like having a meal, going to exercise, going to a meeting, or merely doing another activity. You can expect this project to be more slow-going and should propose your deadlines as such.

If the sections are denser and take more time and mental energy, you should expect to get through fewer sections each day. Ultimately, it is best to take the time you need to make thorough edits of each isolated area, analyze that section, and carefully write down any notes you have instead of trying to power through the text.

Chapter 5: Step 5 - Interacting for Deeper Engagement

One of the best ways to stay engaged with the editing process is to interact with the text. Interacting with the text can take on numerous forms, from making physical marks on punctuation, grammar, and spelling, to taking a creative spin on reading the story from various character's perspectives. As the editor, it is your job to be fully engaged with the texts at all times, sometimes even more than the writer was. Passivity is a grave mistake in an editor and should be avoided at all costs.

The editor must be a reader who can avoid surface level word processing and truly gain something from the text, to offer meaningful feedback in return. In general, interacting with the text helps editors to avoid falling into passive reading and maintain high activity as they go along. This may look like using the imagination, wondering about further possibilities, asking questions, making analyses and evaluations, and otherwise thinking deeply. Through these tactics, editors will have higher levels of comprehension of what they read. Therefore, they will be able to offer more meaningful edits and suggestions to the writer (or make more meaningful edits to their own writing if they are the writer).

Benefits of Deep Text Interaction

There are several benefits to more in-depth interaction with the text in the editing stages, all of which help make the piece of writing as clear, concise, engaging, and error-free as possible. This deeper interaction helps the editor to think deeply about what they are reading and pinpoint when they feel confused or find themselves drifting off. If the editor feels confused at a certain point in the text, that's a good sign that the author needs to re-work that section of text for clarification purposes.

If the editor begins to drift off and has trouble paying attention to the words in front of them, that's a good sign that the writer should move that section of the text, add more colorful language, or remove it entirely. Text interaction helps to fill in any gaps in comprehension and urge the editor to reflect on both what they have taken from the text and what they anticipate for the future.

Physical Interaction Method

The first method of text interaction is physical interaction. This comes through editing methods, which keep the editor's brain engaged in a particular action system. An example of this would be to develop a table of individual edits to apply to punctuation, grammatical, and spelling errors. Perhaps the editor chooses to place an "x" symbol over every area of the text where there is an unnecessary comma, a circle around areas lacking punctuation, three lines under letters that are incorrectly capitalized, and short underlines under words that should be removed or changed. They may choose to underline or bracket the sentences or sections that capture their attention the most and circle the sentences or paragraphs to find themselves feeling lost or bored.

In terms of spelling, if the editor knows a word is misspelled, they may put it in a circle or box, and if they have questions about the spelling or meaning of a word, they may put a question mark. They could also use arrows to indicate where individual sentences should be moved.

Using a physical symbols system keeps the editor's brain on task while they work and helps them keep from getting lost when they try to refer back to the text. It also gives the writer something to look at so they can see all of the places in the text where the editor found issues. This physical interaction provides the editor with something to do as they read, which is enjoyable and useful for keeping the process on track.

Physical interaction is a deliberate act and can be especially helpful if the editor is working with a piece that they do not find naturally attractive or challenging them more than usual. The physical actions may make the task less daunting, and the editor will have more confidence in what they can do.

Personal Interaction Method

Another method of interaction is personal interaction. To do this, the editor may take the approach of building personal connections with the text by relating it to their own experience or understanding of the world. They may engage with the text by asking particular questions of themselves, such as: "How do I feel when I read this scene?" "What are my emotions towards this character?" "Whose side am I on/Who am I rooting for?" "What do I want the outcome of this piece of writing to be?" "Am I pleased with what just happened in this scene?" "What is confusing to me about this scene?" "What have I learned from this piece of writing?" "What new perspective have I gained?".

It's a good idea to make a list of questions such as these for the editor to answer as they go along. By building these personal connections, the editor will begin to feel like there is more at stake for themselves and their personal life. Their interest levels will be higher, and they will be more intentional and less likely to become distracted. Additionally, their answers to these questions should indicate whether or not the writer has done their job.

Every editor should approach their editing projects with the goal of reading to learn. They should comprehensively analyze the text, integrate new ideas and perceptions, and offer feedback that stems from a place of genuine interest and understanding of what the writer wants to convey.

Chapter 6: Step 6 - Letting Things Sit

Most editors have had the experience of growing bored with the piece of writing in front of them and growing exhausted from reading the same characters, dialogues, and scenes over and over again. This is called burnout, and as an editor, you can almost certainly expect it to happen to you. Editing can be a tedious process, especially once you're a few editing passes in. This is a natural and normal part of the process, but it is not productive. Once you have reached this point, the best way to get back on track is to grant yourself time to step away. Go out and live your life for a few hours, a day, or a few days, without having to think about the editing project at hand. Give yourself a chance to read, engage with other things you enjoy, relax, watch the people and things going on around you, and gain some fresh perspective.

When you come back to the editing process, you can do so with "fresh eyes" and a new perspective for the content in front of you. With this fresh perspective, you will not only enjoy the process more and feel more energized; you will also be able to catch things you did not notice before and offer new critiques. In some cases, you may even find yourself suggesting the writer bring in an entirely new idea or change the focus of individual sections entirely.

Choosing to Take a Break When Frustrated

Looking over the same piece of writing over and over can cause the work to become stale. No editor is unfamiliar with the feeling that comes when you're sitting at your desk, looking at the same project, and nothing is coming forth. Although you know you should have more to say and that there are undoubtedly more edits to make, nothing is coming to you. It is expected that you will start to feel tired throughout the editing process and have trouble focusing as you read the same section for the third or fourth time. You may find yourself beginning to feel frustrated and not know how much more you can do. You may also be dealing with a flustered writer (or, perhaps, you are this flustered writer) who just can't seem to find what "works."

Frustration is usually a good sign that it is time to take a step back. If you find yourself losing sight of the purpose of the writing and the enjoyment in the process of editing it, you will benefit the most from giving yourself a break. If you feel like you have to force yourself through every page, give yourself space from the text to think about what isn't working, get back in touch with your creativity, restore your energy, and bring back some fresh ideas.

Choosing to take a break can save you hours of staring at a screen or page and not comprehending any of the words in front of you. When you take a step back, take some time to remind yourself of the writer's (or your own) purpose in writing this piece. Ask yourself, "What's the point?" and give yourself time to meditate on that while you take a break from it. It's also important not to make yourself miserable throughout the writing process. If you start to feel yourself continuously wrapped up in negative emotions from the stress of editing, do yourself a favor and give yourself some time to rest, breathe, and do things that bring you joy.

Tuning into Your Surroundings

One method for giving your editing space while still gathering perspectives, which will be beneficial when you return, is to tune in to your surroundings when you go out. While you are taking your break from editing, pay particular attention to the people you see around you at the grocery store, in the park, at the mall, or on the streets.

Watch the way they interact with each other; note the way they use body language and the way they engage in daily dialogue. Suppose you're editing a piece of writing that involves character dialogue. In that case, you can take inspiration from the real world to see if the dialogue you're editing sounds realistic and flows well or if it sounds unnatural and hard to follow. As you listen to everyday people engage in conversation, you may realize that some of the dialogue in the piece you're editing sounds too formal or boring. The natural world is full of inspiration, and taking a break to simply inhabit the world can be revolutionary to your editing style.

Strengthening Character Development from Real-World People

This observation of everyday people can also give you more insight to offer the writer on how to develop their characters. You may have the idea of realistic descriptions to add to a particular character to make them seem more relatable, an action they can take that would surprise the reader, etc. You may even have an idea for a new character goal, or a new character entirely, which you can present to the writer (or bring into the piece yourself if you are the writer). Observing a couple in love on a park bench, the exact way they touch each other, how they move their heads to look at each other, and how they speak could form the way you reframe such a circumstance as you edit the writing.

You may see an older woman in the supermarket who reminds you of one of the characters in the piece you are editing. You can take down some brief observations to bring into her character description to become more realistic. As you discreetly observe body language and general human interactions, you may be able to provide further tips for the writer to create scenes the readers can visualize and relate to. The more the reader can visually see what is happening and establish a sense of interest and relatability with the characters, the more inclined they will be to continue reading.

You can play into this interest level by relating the characters in the work you're editing to people you see in your everyday life. If you are editing a piece of writing that involves a motorcyclist named Haven, for example, and you see a woman in a café who rides a motorcycle and reminds you of how the character of Haven may be in real life, you can draw inspiration from the way she drinks her coffee, the tattoos on her arms, etc. In this way, simple observation of real human beings can revolutionize character development and improvement in the editing stage.

Reading for Other Purposes

Another essential thing to do while taking your break from editing is to engage with other author's writing. In many cases, you cannot engage with work you are editing as you would if it were merely a book you picked up off the shelf. The content may be something that is not interesting to you, or you may simply not be able to feel interested because you have too much work to do with finding errors and making suggestions. For this reason, it is crucial always to have something you are reading for pure enjoyment and learning, rather than editing.

As you read the work of other authors you enjoy, ask yourself questions like, "What about this piece of writing captures my attention, and how does the author maintain it?" "Do I care about the characters in this story? If so, why do I care? If not, why not?" "How does the author keep this story moving forward and keep me from becoming bored?" You can improve your editing skills drastically by understanding the techniques used by the authors you like and making similar suggestions to the authors you work with (or applying them to your writing). If you or the author feel like the piece of writing needs something more but can't progress beyond where it is, you can use other writers' work to remind yourself how to bring in extra elements that maintain reader interest.

Move the Mind, Move the Body

Most writers and editors will tell you that moving the body is crucial, especially when your brain is constantly active. Sometimes, your thoughts will become so chaotic and activated that they don't know where to go, and it can become hard to continue the editing process in this state. Mental and physical activity go hand in hand, and you indeed cannot have one without the other. Exercise keeps our brains clear, our moods positive, and our emotions even, which are all critical throughout the editing process's challenges. In many cases, sitting down to edit after a workout is excellent because your mind will be crystal clear, your endorphins will be freely flowing, and you will likely feel more in control and ready to tackle your task.

Editing is a stressful process, and exercise is the perfect way to release that buildup of stress. This doesn't need to get a gym membership or join the community sand volleyball league; it merely means you need to find the way that works best for you to move your body and use it (especially during the editing process). In many cases, a nice jog, yoga practice, dance workout video, or walk around the neighborhood can be the perfect release of endorphins and a way to refocus your brain for when you come back to editing. Whatever type of exercise it takes for you to release your stress, clear your head, and revive your energy, give yourself time to step away and do it.

Giving Yourself Adequate Time

In every step of the editing process, it is important to give yourself plenty of time. If you rush your deadlines and set crunched timelines for yourself, you will not be able to be as clear-headed and thorough. Ultimately, this will result in a less refined piece of writing. While it is easy to become so caught up in the editing process that you feel desperate just to get it done, this can pose a great threat to the work's quality. Be sure not to short yourself on time. Editing is a process that cannot be rushed, and you need to allow for plenty of space to take breaks to make the most intentional edits possible. If you're wondering how long your breaks should be or how much time you should request to meet your editing deadlines, remember that the writing will ultimately benefit from any space you take away from it.

Try your best to keep guilty feelings at bay and value your own time, energy, and general enjoyment in the process. If you are editing for another writer, it is important to have a transparent conversation with them about the importance of breaks and taking space from the writing. Clarify your needs and why you are setting a particular deadline. This will help the author understand your process, which will ultimately put less pressure on you and allow you to do your absolute best.

Redirecting Energy on the "Off Days"

If you sit down to write one day and you feel overwhelmed by negative emotions, lack of motivation, or general disinterest, it's probably not a day you should be writing. In a society that is very driven towards production and meeting deadlines, it's hard to believe it would be okay to change your plans on a day you planned to edit. However, if you don't feel like this is the right day for you to do hours of editing, it probably isn't.

With good planning, you can provide this flexibility for yourself. It's okay for today not to be the right day to edit the way you planned. Instead, decide how you're going to spend the day giving yourself a break, re-cultivating your interest, and drawing interest from the world around you. Just because you're not doing the editing in your traditional process doesn't mean you can't gain experience from reading, taking notes of the things you observe in the world around you, and giving yourself time for the things you need and the things that bring you relaxation and joy. Editing is a draining process, and the more drained you become, the less quality work you will perform. If you sit down and realize today isn't the day for editing, allow yourself to step away, redirecting that energy to a place where it can be productive, then come back tomorrow.

Planning Breaks Ahead of Time

On a typical editing day, it's not a good idea to sit down for hours at a time and try to get everything done. If you do this, your brain may become desensitized to issues with style or other edits that need to be made and start automatically filling in the gaps that need your attention. If you plan to write for four hours, it's a good idea to decide how long your breaks will be within that period. Even if you take just five minutes every hour to stand up, stretch, drink some water, or step outside for a breath of air, your writing process will thank you immensely. You may also try an approach where you write for several hours a day for two days, then take a day to step away. In some cases, however, you may need even longer. Deadlines permitting, you may need to step away for several weeks or even months.

This is especially useful if you are trying to edit your writing and find yourself hitting walls. Give yourself time to live your life, and during that time, you'll be surprised at the new observations, perspective, and energy to bring back to the editing process when you're ready.

Chapter 7: Step 7 - Editing in Reverse

Let's say you have read and edited the same piece of writing several times, and you're beginning to hit a wall. You know that there is more to do, but you can't quite figure it out. You have indicated the writer's main goals, determined where the tension and crisis points are, paid attention to the momentum at various points throughout, made basic grammatical, spelling, and punctuation edits, checked for consistency and clarity, and even read the manuscript aloud. All of the standard editing boxes are checked, yet you still feel that something is missing. This is where editing in reverse comes in.

Overcoming Preconceptions, Deepening Concentration

As discussed previously, your brain automatically fills in the gaps as you edit. When it isn't necessary to focus on every word to get the text's main point, it's common to miss places where the flow is not as smooth as it should be, words are misspelled, or faulty punctuation is used. Putting things in reverse (meaning starting with the last sentence and making your way up) helps to hone your focus on each word and sentence in a new way.

Editing in reverse forces your brain to confront what feels like entirely new information. You will have to slow down and read each word and sentence as if it is the first time you've ever seen it. In many ways, it is the first time you've ever seen it because by reading in a different order, you are automatically unable to operate under the same unconscious assumptions of the plot. The more comfortable you are with the flow of the story and the plot, the more likely you'll be to miss problem areas. Reading in reverse allows you to disrupt this comfort, go against your unconscious assumptions, and genuinely engage with the text with fresh eyes.

When you start from the end, your brain can't assume that "we already know all this," and you will therefore be able to be much more thorough. Each paragraph you read will become an entity that stands alone, which allows you to be more intentional as you examine the sentence structure and words. As you read more slowly and with greater intention and challenge, you will be more deliberate in your editing. Your concentration will deepen, and you will notice the flow of each paragraph in a way you did not before.

Beginning at the End

When you begin the process of editing in reverse, you will want to start at the very end of the manuscript. You may choose to read the pages in the standard order, from top to bottom, but you can read from bottom to top if you want an even more significant editing challenge. By taking each page and paragraph out of context you have become familiar with, you will have to look at each word and phrase and ask yourself what it accomplishes. You will want to make corrections as you go, marking up the paper or making notes in the margins. If you have a new idea for a sentence structure, try it out in the margins. If you're not sure about a correction, feel free to indicate your uncertainty using parentheses or a question mark so you can refer back later on in the editing process.

As you move through the paragraphs, you may choose to choose some method of indicating that you have finished a paragraph, so you don't look at again until the next editing pass. You may highlight a section, mark it with an asterisk, or something else of the sort.

Correcting Consistency, Punctuation, Grammar, and Spelling

Editing in reverse gives you more ability to identify inconsistencies within the text. You may find, for example, that a character is present in a scene they shouldn't be in, or perhaps that a scene is placed in the wrong order. You're more likely to catch these things if you're reading the text in a different way than you're used to. Some of the other things you'll be looking for in the reverse editing stage are punctuation, spelling, and grammar errors.

Identifying Overuse

However, there are several other emphasis areas you should keep in mind, as well. The first of these is the overuse of certain words. Every writer has words they overuse, which can cause the manuscript to lose its flavor. As you read through the manuscript in reverse, highlight, or underline every time the writer uses a similar word. Perhaps they overuse the adjective "beautiful", or the phrase "That being said." After identifying the overused words and phrases, you can easily use a Google search or another simple tool to identify supplementary words and phrases the writer could use instead.

Identifying "Non" Words

Another thing to look out for in the reverse editing process is the use of "non" words. These are the words that can easily be removed without changing anything about the sentence meaning. In many cases, these words are "dead" to the sentence, meaning they make it less impactful and break the flow. There are thousands of "non" words out there, with the words "just," "really," and "very" being just a few.

Drafting in Reverse

In addition to editing in reverse, many editors also find it helpful to draft a reverse outline to check the work. The process of reversal outlining involves taking away all supporting evidence and details and leaving yourself with only the writer's main ideas. You should be able to define these main ideas using bullet-points, which you should ensure are placed in a logical order. This provides a condensed version of the piece of writing, in which the writer can confront if all of their goals have genuinely been met in their main points. After you

172

have generated a reverse outline of the main points you gathered in the editing process, the writer will better understand the places where they need to provide more evidence, expand or condense a scene, or move things around for better organization.

Keeping Author Goals in Mind

The reverse outline cannot be created until the writer has completed a draft and provided it to you to describe their goals. Once you are aware of the goals, you can proceed through the manuscript with a sense of alertness about what is being accomplished in each chapter and paragraph. Before you begin editing, ask the author to present you with a basic outline that lists their writing's main ideas as they understand them. This outline will serve as something to refer back to throughout the editing process and give you something to question. As you begin making your reverse outline, consider using numbers with each bulleted point to keep yourself on track with which paragraph or chapter talks about what.

Answering Crucial Questions

The most critical point of a reverse outline is to answer questions. As you go through each paragraph, section, or chapter, ask yourself if they accurately relate to the author's expressed goals. This strategy will help you catch any scenes or pieces of information that seem irrelevant to the big picture and end up de-railing readers. As you proceed throughout the reverse outlining process, you may find yourself confronting new topics or ideas which are presented throughout the paper and may not relate to the main idea. In this case, the author either needs to change the main idea of the writing itself or remove the irrelevant information.

Another question you should ask yourself throughout the reverse outlining process is where the reader may have trouble feeling on track with the points' order. Are there areas where they may be confused chronologically or feel that they need more information? By asking this question, you can make editing suggestions for how the writer might rearrange the manuscript or individual paragraphs themselves to keep the reader feeling on track and tied into the writing's central theme(s).

As you examine each paragraph, make sure that you do not have any sections repeating the same idea. Although each paragraph should be relevant to the main idea, they should all say something new. If you have two paragraphs saying almost the same thing, it will help combine them, remove one, or revise so that they are each making a different point.

Editing the Specifics of Each Paragraph

It is also essential to make sure that each paragraph stays focused on a single topic. The writer should not try to cover too much ground in a single section; if they do, the reader will more easily get lost. If you identify paragraphs which try to tackle too many things, suggest that the writer separate those ideas to form further paragraphs, or cut the information out if it is not entirely relevant. Lastly, check each section for length requirements. Are they too long or too short? An excellent way to gauge this is by looking at the total number of pages. The longer the piece of writing, the less of a problem it is to have a few longer paragraphs. That said, it is vital to check each paragraph in-depth to make sure that it fits with the flow of the rest of the piece.

Conclusion

When you started this guide, you likely approached it as either the editor of another writer's work or with the desire to edit your writing thoroughly. You picked up this guide with the understanding that in-depth editing is crucial to the overall success of the piece that is being written and that errors in structure, clarity, punctuation, grammar, dialogue, and flow can have a drastically negative impact on how others receive your writing. You were likely aware of all that is at stake in the editing process, especially when it comes to maintaining the interest, understanding, and general respect of readers.

No matter how incredible a story's content is, too many spelling errors, grammatical mistakes, or inconsistencies can ruin the whole experience for a reader. When it comes to the editing stage, you must come prepared for the fact that how thorough you edit the book can make or break the levels of respect, and subsequent sales, it will have. When you edit your work, you should do so not only to create work you can be truly proud of, but also to cultivate a community of followers who have a deep respect for the work you produce.

Throughout the guide, you were provided with the ins and outs of the editing process, from the structural, line editing, and copywriting stages, to the importance of reading aloud, to the seemingly minor details of formatting, to deeply engaging with the content to a point where you can ensure reader impact. You became aware of the risks of missing small pieces if you become careless, and you learned how to be more thorough when it comes to catching these small pieces before it's too late.

You were provided with tips for keeping yourself engaged and present with the work you do. You also learned the benefits of creating a network of friends, followers, trusted writers, and perhaps other editors into your editing process for extra support and perspective. You learned how to maintain a fresh perspective while honoring your own energy by taking breaks, giving the writing space to breathe, taking inspiration from your surroundings, editing in reverse, and creating reverse outlines to clarify the author's main points.

You discovered the importance of being thorough and conducting as many editing passes as necessary to get the writing as close to perfect as possible. You were shown the benefits of reading work aloud to yourself and other people, because hearing it in your own voice can bring attention to details that are easy to skip while reading. You learned how to isolate parts of the text to scan for clarity and cohesivity, as well as how to step outside the original context of the text to slow down and hone in on the smaller details. Additionally, you came to understand some of the best editors' secrets and how to monitor your text for efficiency and full reader engagement.

At the end of the guide, you were provided with fresh ways to work with the text at hand to keep yourself alert and conscious of changes that still need to be made. This will help you save from being burnt out and becoming careless with your editing process. The better job you do as an editor, the more the reader will enjoy their engagement with it, and the more they will search for future pieces by you (or the writer you are editing for) in the future. No matter where you are on your editing journey, this guide is guaranteed to serve as the tool you need to keep yourself on track!

More by Jaiden Pemton

Discover all books from the Creative Writing Series by Jaiden Pemton at:

bit.ly/jaiden-pemton

Book 1: *How to Write Fiction*

Book 2: *How to Tell a Story*

Book 3: *How to Write a Screenplay*

Book 4: *How to Write Sales Copy*

Book 5: *How to Edit Writing*

Book 6: *How to Self-Publish*

Book 7: *How to Write Non-Fiction*

Book 8: *How to Write Content*

Themed book bundles available at discounted prices:

bit.ly/jaiden-pemton

www.ingramcontent.com/pod-product-compliance
Lightning Source LLC
Chambersburg PA
CBHW050342160726
48002CB00001B/423